THE ECONOMICS
OF
FOREIGN EXCHANGE

THE ECONOMICS
OF
FOREIGN
EXCHANGE

A practical market approach

NICK DOUCH

Q

QUORUM BOOKS
New York · Westport, Connecticut

Published in the United States and Canada by
Quorum Books, Westport, Connecticut

English language edition, except the United States and Canada,
published by Woodhead-Faulkner (Publishers) Ltd.

First published 1989

Library of Congress Cataloging-in-Publication Data
Douch, Nick.
    The economics of foreign exchange.
    1. Foreign exchange   I. Title.
HG3821.D74   1989   332.4'5   89-4033
ISBN 0-89930-499-0 (lib. bdg. : alk. paper)

Copyright © 1989 by Nick Douch

Library of Congress Catalog Card Number: 89-4033

ISBN: 0-89930-499-0

Printed in Great Britain

CONTENTS

ACKNOWLEDGEMENTS

Several people have helped me enormously in the writing of this book. Paul Sanderson gave me many of the ideas which were turned into the 'theory' chapters, but the interpretation of these ideas was mine, so errors are firmly of my own making.

Steven Duffy spent time and trouble preparing data for the tables and graphs which punctuate the chapters. I am also very grateful to Barclays Bank Economics Department for allowing me to use their data in the book.

Jim Cunningham, Richard Froud, and especially Chris Wright spent many hours sorting out some quite hideous errors in my first draft, but even their super-human efforts cannot be expected to pick up every mistake that I made, so once again those that remain are my own responsibility.

Finally I should like to thank all those colleagues at Barclays Hofex (now Global Treasury Services), London who have worked with me over the last few years. It is only by watching their professionalism that I have been able to begin to understand how the foreign exchange market really works.

INTRODUCTION

The idea behind this book is an attempt to blend economic theory with practical reality, or, at least if not to blend the two, to compare and contrast them. To non-participants in the foreign exchange market, exchange rates often seem to move in mystical and unexpected ways, sometimes bearing no relation to the underlying economic forces that are meant to dictate which currencies are strong and which are weak.

Indeed, many a politician or central bank has said that exchange markets bear no relation to reality (a statement most often made when their own currency is going in a direction that was either unanticipated or undesired!). Nevertheless, when the market is moving their currency in the 'right' direction these same politicians may be heard to extol its virtues in setting exchange rates.

This book comprises four main parts. Part I examines five different economic approaches to exchange rate movements. Some would argue that all these approaches stem from the same source – that of the effect of inflation differentials on economic performance and hence on the exchange rate. Yet this would do them a dis-service. Derivatives they may be, but each adds to our understanding of the rationale behind exchange rate movements, and while none could be described as the authoritative theory of exchange rate movements, each is worth examining to see what can be gleaned, stored and used for future exchange rate predictions.

Part II consists of two quite short chapters. The first examines the advantages of fixed and floating exchange rates – an area of discussion that is once again returning to the forefront of politicians' minds (particularly those in G-7 or in the European Economic Community). The second looks at a brief history of exchange rate regimes since the Second World War, and in particular the Bretton Woods Agreement. This may seem an odd place for a chapter on the history of exchange rates, but it provides a good link between the theories of Part I and the practical realities of Part II.

In the first three chapters of Part III we consider how the spot and forward exchange rate markets actually work. By this I mean the motives of the market participants – I do not suggest that this solves the mysteries of the workings of the two markets. Chapter 11 takes a brief look at ways in which game theory might be used to explain some of the shenanigans in the market, and I admit to being attracted to this idea. But although the concept is not fully developed here, the ideas are well worth pondering.

Chapter 12 looks at the effect of new foreign exchange hedging instruments on the market. Most stress is placed on the seller of the instrument, for it is with the seller that most of the increased foreign exchange activity will lie. There follows a chapter on chart analysis, and although I remain agnostic as to its efficacy, no book on the foreign exchange market would be complete without reference to an area which is seen by many as the only worthwhile method of forecasting exchange rate movements – or at least very short-term ones.

Finally, Chapter 14 attempts to tie the whole book together by examining when economic theories and forecasts are helpful in predicting exchange rates, and, perhaps even more importantly, when they are not.

There is a long appendix which defines various economic indicators, and seeks to explain how the market might react to them and why. It is written very much from the viewpoint of a dealer rather than from that of an economist. It may well be considered cynical by the latter, particularly when it suggests that the interpretation by the market may well be different at different times.

This is not a theoretical book on foreign exchange models. Rather, it is a book written by someone who has worked closely with the foreign exchange market, but who has had an economist's training. I understand the relevance of economics in the exchange markets, but I am frustrated by its inadequacies in forecasting the future. There are reasons for this, and it is to these reasons that the latter part of the book turns. Knowing these reasons (or at least some of them) helps, but it will never completely remove the frustration.

Part I

THEORIES OF EXCHANGE RATE MOVEMENT

1

PURCHASING POWER PARITY

Introduction

There is something intuitively convincing about the idea that an increase in prices in one country which outstrips the increase in another country should lead to a weakening in the exchange rate of the country with the higher price increases, such as to bring the relative price of goods back to an equilibrium position. Such a proposition seems little more than common sense, and it is hardly surprising that it is put forward as a theory for determining exchange rate movements. However, though this proposition may be intuitively simple, proving it in practice is a problem of a different dimension altogether.

The definition of purchasing power parity

Purchasing power parity proceeds from the notion that at some point there is an equilibrium level of exchange rate which equates the price of externally traded goods in one country with the price of those goods in another country. If price increases in the goods are the same in both countries, there will be no change in the exchange rate because, relatively speaking, the value of each currency has not changed – although of course if there is inflation, both currencies will have changed in absolute value, and both will be worth less by the same amount against some third currency. If, however, the rates of price increases in the two countries are different, then the condition of relative value will break down, and the exchange rate must change to restore the equilibrium position. The currency with the higher inflation rate will have lost value relatively faster, and the exchange rate will worsen by the ratio of the two inflation rates.

$$\text{change in exchange rate} = \frac{\text{change in inflation rate in country A}}{\text{change in inflation rate in country B}}$$

It is obvious of course that the change cannot be instantaneous, and that variations will occur as equilibrium is sought. Nevertheless, over a period of time the new equilibrium position will be reached. However, even with this added subtlety, there are many other difficulties in using this system, and over the years the system has been added to and refined.

The origins of puchasing power parity

The Gold Standard, which had predominated in the setting of currency rates up to the First World War, had always been a self-correcting mechanism for currencies when operated continuously. However, the Gold Standard could not remedy the situation caused by the hiatus of the War. In particular, if currencies were to be relinked to the Gold Standard at what level should this be? Something had to be devised to define changes in the various economies in the intervening years so that starting points between currencies would be accurate. From this need the first ideas of purchasing power parity grew. It seemed reasonable to consider the growth in prices in each economy relative to the others to establish how a particular currency should be devalued by inflation relative to other currencies.

History tells us that the attempts to return to the Gold Standard were not successful, a good example being sterling. With the benefit of hindsight it is easy to see where the theorists went wrong. Advice to the Chancellor of the time, Winston Churchill, was that since wholesale prices had increased in roughly the same proportion in both the UK and the USA, it was reasonable to link the pound to the Gold Standard at the same rate as it had been relative to the dollar before the First World War.

It soon became clear that the rate was much too high and that British goods were uncompetitive in world markets. In fact, by using wholesale prices which had a large volume of internationally traded raw materials and commodities where there was an international clearing price, the increase in UK prices was grossly understated. It became clear that one of the major problems in establishing purchasing power parity was the increase in the price of non-traded goods (i.e. those which cannot be exported or imported). These, by their very nature, were much more difficult to relate from one country or currency to another.

Problems of calculating purchasing power parity

Apart from traded and non-traded goods making life difficult when trying to calculate the correct exchange rate for purchasing power parity, there are a number of other factors which can create even greater problems.

1. The starting point

If we are to make sensible suggestions as to how currencies should change in response to changes in price levels, then it is obviously vital to establish a point at which currencies were last in equilibrium. In the days of the Gold Standard this was not too difficult, but in a world of floating exchange rates, with both high and ever-changing currency volatility, it is far from easy to establish what such a point might be. Indeed many of the controversies associated with the definition of the correct levels of currencies, or exchange rates at which a particular currency is competitive, are derived from this problem. One's starting point will determine where one ends because: first the absolute starting point may differ for different observers, and second, the rate at which one has calculated the relative price changes could alter. This problem may well be insoluble but there is worse to come.

2. Trade barriers

Puchasing power parity must suppose a world where trade can be freely conducted, otherwise an international clearing price could never be constructed. In reality, we have nothing of the sort. There are innumerable barriers which are direct in that they either restrict volumes of imports or impose duties of one sort or another, or are hidden by regulations which, if sufficiently detailed, give home producers a decided edge over foreign producers. It is not the purpose of this book to comment on the desirability or otherwise of trade barriers. However, their imposition does mean that the size of the traded goods sector is reduced relative to the non-traded goods sector. This can only mean that the distortions to price changes are even greater.

3. Changes in the pattern of demand and output

A further implicit assumption behind purchasing power parity is that the pattern of expenditure on goods remains the same over the period in question. In other words consumption is not affected by new inventions or developments. This seems unlikely and in this case, there would be a risk, if not a certainty, that the price indices would become out of date and would fail to reflect changes in the commodity composition of demand and output, and that they would thus not provide an accurate guide to purchasing power. For example, the introduction of the television set and – closer to the present time – the computer, clearly had an impact on what people spent their money on. Yet this major change in people's consumption patterns would not generally be reflected in any calculation of purchasing power parity. However, even if the price indices are continually reweighted to take account of these changes, there must inevitably be a lag between the change in demand and the change in weighting.

4. *Different tastes between economies*

It is highly unlikely that the views of consumers in one economy will be the same as those in another when it comes to prioritising items on which to spend their incomes. There will be a wide variety of different tastes and a great disparity between what can be described as necessities and what can be thought of as luxuries. This must mean that the demand for goods will vary from country to country, and the effect of changing the price may not be the same from one country to the next. In other words, the elasticity of demand for a given good will differ from one economy to another. In these circumstances it becomes difficult to determine the effect on different patterns of expenditure of a given price increase, and the effect this will have on the overall price level in two different economies. In these circumstances it becomes difficult to calculate where purchasing power parity is.

5. *Which price indices to use*

There is a wide variety of price indices available which vary from the very wide gross domestic product (GDP) deflator through consumer prices to wholesale prices. There are also different measures for imports and exports, so that it is difficult to say which is the correct measure to use when comparing relative prices.

Consumer prices are one popular attempt at comparison, but in recent years certain economies – notably that of Japan – have been able to insulate, to a great extent, the price of their exports from the impact of domestic cost changes. It can be argued that using consumer prices in this case will lead to the establishing of purchasing power parity at too low levels of the yen, and that Japanese exports could still compete in world markets at higher levels of the yen.

If, instead, we consider export prices as being the more accurate index because these are a better example of what is going on in international trade, it would be equally relevant to use the index of import prices. The two are of course not the antithesis of each other, because the mix of imports from different countries will differ from one economy to another.

All would be fine if all the indices moved even approximately in line with each other, or that the differences averaged out over a period, but as can be seen from the Table 1.1 which uses the UK as an example, this is not true. Thus the correct choice of index may be just one more insoluble problem.

6. *Taxes*

Taxes are likely to vary between countries not only in their levels, but also in the way in which they are levied: they may be direct or indirect; they may be levied

Table 1.1 United Kingdom inflation: annual percentage changes

Year	Retail price inflation (RPI)	Producer price inflation (PPI) input	(PPI) output	Average earnings	Gross domestic product deflator	Export prices
1975	24.3	11.8	23.1	26.6	27.3	22.7
1976	16.6	24.6	16.2	15.6	14.6	19.6
1977	15.8	15.4	18.2	10.2	14.0	18.4
1978	8.3	3.4	9.9	14.6	11.1	9.5
1979	13.4	13.0	10.9	15.3	14.5	10.8
1980	18.0	8.5	14.0	18.8	19.8	14.3
1981	11.9	9.2	9.6	13.4	11.5	8.8
1982	8.6	7.3	7.7	11.4	7.7	7.2
1983	4.6	6.9	5.4	8.6	5.1	7.8
1984	5.1	8.1	6.2	5.7	4.1	8.2
1985	6.1	1.1	5.6	11.2	5.8	5.1
1986	3.4	−7.6	4.5	8.3	3.7	−4.2
1987	4.2	3.1	3.8	8.0	4.5	3.6

on income or expenditure; they may be of a current or capital nature, and there may be significant tax breaks which allow taxes to be legally avoided.

All these differences will cause distortions in the economy. For example, they will obviously alter the level of price changes of individual goods, and will thus have an influence on changes in the overall level of prices. It could be argued, therefore, that the effects of tax should be removed from price indices when assessing purchasing power parity.

However, the effect of taxes will have a significant effect on demand patterns. A good example of this was faster than inflationary tax rises on cigarettes in the UK, which together with health fears have led to falls in consumption. Thus to use price indices net of taxes would not show how the price increases affect the buyer.

Summary
All the above problems have to do with measuring purchasing power parity, and while they make it very difficult to research the relationship statistically, they do not necessarily invalidate the theory. Are there, however, problems that might cast doubt on the efficacy of the whole idea?

The direction of causality

If it seems intuitively correct to assume that changes in relative price levels will have an effect on exchange rate levels, it seems equally plausible to assume that changes in exchange rate levels will have an effect on relative price levels. The implication here is that the demand for a good is elastic, and that changes in prices will have an unequivocal effect on demand for that good. In reality there are many goods for which the assumption of elasticity is certainly not valid, at least in the short run. When the Organisation of the Petroleum Exporting Countries (OPEC) quadrupled the price of oil in the 1970s, there was no immediate rein on demand, for the simple reason that no substitute for oil could be found sufficiently quickly. Higher oil prices certainly depressed demand by squeezing out marginal businesses and spending decisions, and encouraged speedier research into alternative forms of energy; but in the short run most consumers simply had to grit their teeth, make marginal savings, but watch their costs soar.

In itself the rise in oil prices was not a case of exchange rates increasing inflation. However, oil, like many commodities, is priced in US dollars, and when the latter currency began to soar in the early 1980s, the price of raw material inputs to non-dollar currencies rose sharply. This obviously had an impact on inflation, causing it to rise, and cause and effect were the reverse of that suggested in purchasing power parity. The higher inflation so caused could of course lead to the exchange rate depreciating further as relative price levels have changed, which in turn may mean that the lower currency level will cause higher inflation, and so on.

Determination of the direction of causality seems unlikely to be a simple solution, which must cast some doubt on the worth of purchasing power parity in its strictest form, but does it mean that the whole construct needs to be thrown out of the window?

Instantaneous or gradual adjustment

The strictest form of model using purchasing power parity assumes that the exchange rate will always take immediate account of the effect of the change in relative price levels. All the problems discussed above suggest that this is unlikely. In addition there are many practical reasons why the changes should not happen immediately. These range from the fact that goods are often delivered under fixed price contracts of some length, to the fact that rises in input prices may not be able to be passed on because of demand and competitive constraints. Purists might argue that these are really faults of the price data, but this seems a semantic argument. If a theory cannot be proved, its worth for predicting is greatly reduced.

More fundamentally, it appears that exchange rates can be affected by outside shocks, when the supply of or demand for a country's goods are changed in a way that overwhelms any price effect. An example of this would be the discovery of North Sea oil which led to a vast increase in the supply of UK goods available for export. The demand for sterling to buy this oil obviously meant that the equilibrium between the supply and demand for the pound was disturbed, and in the absence of any immediate countervailing shock this would lead to a rise in the exchange rate of sterling, which over a period of time did of course happen. In fact, over the period of sterling's rise, the inflation rate in the UK was higher than that of most of its trading partners, which on purchasing power parity grounds alone would have led to a fall in the pound. It would thus seem sensible to allow for these shocks and to suggest that purchasing power parity is in fact a long-term condition for exchange rate stability, and that significant deviations from the expected equilibrium are likely and allowable while this long-term adjustment is taking place. In other words the adjustment to relative price levels is gradual.

Can these shocks be incorporated into the theory?

The problem with recognising shocks and their effects on the exchange rate is that they are always much easier to spot after the event. In other words it is much easier to explain why the US dollar was rising sharply in the early 1980s when the country was already running a trade deficit, since it is now obvious that capital flows were sufficient to overcome the current account outflow. The inflow of capital, however, was not so much a vote of confidence by overseas investors in the US economy under President Reagan; rather, it was a reduction in outflows of capital by US residents who saw better opportunities at home. However, while this analysis now looks very plausible, at the time it was much less easy to spot, and most commentators looked to explain it by inflows of overseas funds responding to the high level of US interest rates and to President Reagan's economic policies.

The problem is that shocks have a nasty habit of being unique, not only because of their effect on the exchange rate, but also because of the type of shock. Technological breakthroughs, for example, are likely to be different from anything that has gone before, and their future effect on the economy can be little more than supposition. Thus although external shocks can be incorporated, they are much better used to explain past events – an important exercise in the foreign exchange market – than to predict future movements in exchange rates.

If, then, purchasing power parity as a theory can always be distorted by other events, does it have any use at all in predicting where exchange rates should be?

Do relative prices between economies have any relevance for exchange rate movements?

Even if we assume some two-way causality between exchange rate movements and inflation rates, the evidence of long-run statistics is that there is a sufficiently close relationship between relative inflation rates and exchange rates for relative inflation rates to be a cause of exchange rate movements.

The scatter diagram in Fig. 1.1 plots the average exchange rate change for the last ten years (against the US dollar) on one axis, and on the other the average inflation differential between that country and the USA. The diagram shows a good degree of correlation and, even allowing for an unmeasurable degree of 'reverse causality', it seems likely that on a long-term basis there is an effect.

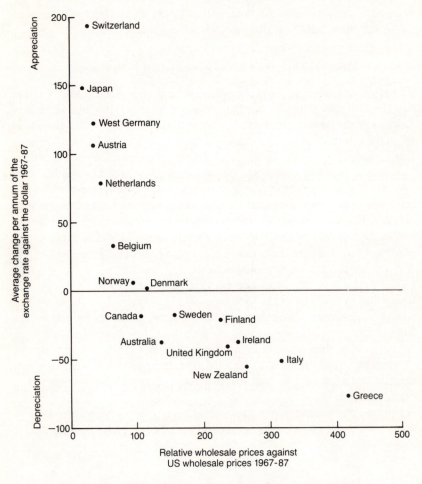

Fig. 1.1 Scatter diagram of exchange rate changes plotted against inflation differentials

To this should be added the idea outlined at the beginning of this chapter, that it seems very likely, on common-sense grounds if nothing else, that relative prices should influence exchange rate movements. However, it is also clear from much of the work done on the subject since floating exchange rates were introduced that there is much less correlation between relative price changes and exchange rate movements in the short term. This is hardly surprising given the volatility of the last few years, and it seems almost certain that exchange rates will move for other reasons and not just because of relative prices.

Thus purchasing power parity should not be used for predicting short-term movements in exchange rates. Its use is of most value in determining whether a currency's current position bears any relation to the long-term equilibrium position. Obviously, if a currency is experiencing persistently high inflation, and its exchange rate remains stable or becomes stronger, then the position is gradually becoming more and more unstable.

However, seemingly 'wrong' trends can continue for some time; indeed for much longer than would seem possible. Purchasing power parity can highlight those currencies whose position is becoming more and more unstable, but it can tell us very little about the precise moment at which the currency will turn, or about how the path to a more stable future will go, and it cannot tell us whether the adjustment will be gradual or abrupt.

Conclusion

Purchasing power parity could almost be said to be the Grand Old Man of currency explanations, but for all its age and its manifest weaknesses, it still plays a major part in assessing the strains between different currencies. Where there is a fixed exchange rate system – such as the European Monetary System (EMS) – short-term volatility is reduced and inflation differentials can provide guidance on which currencies are likely to be revalued and which currencies are likely to be devalued at any realignment, but purchasing power parity still cannot tell us the precise moment of the realignment.

In floating exchange rate systems, short-term volatility seems to overpower everything else, and on this basis purchasing power parity is a poor indicator. However, through all the 'noise' of short-term movements, longer trends can be identified, and it is here that the theory clearly scores.

2

THE BALANCE OF PAYMENTS
APPROACH

As the foreign exchange rate is the relative price of two currencies, so this price will be determined by the supply and demand for each currency on the world's foreign exchanges. If only it were possible to determine these relative supplies and demands exactly, then it would be easy to determine what the equilibrium price would be – or at least should be!

The balance of payments measures the flows across the exchanges and is therefore a measure of supply and demand. However, there are many difficulties – not least measurement ones – in calculating what the actual balance of payments flows are at any stage of time. Nevertheless, on commonsense grounds it seems highly likely that the balance of payments – or some part thereof – plays a part in determining the exchange rate. Over the years a number of approaches have been developed to look at this area.

The balance of trade

The balance of trade is the balance struck after the export and import of goods. It thus includes such items as raw materials, finished products and agricultural goods. However, it does not include 'invisibles', which include payment for services, tourism, interest payments, dividend payments, and government transfers – both outward and inward. It is difficult to believe that, in a well-developed economy, the impact on the exchange rate of a deficit on the balance on invisible trade should be any different from the impact of a deficit on invisible trade. Most approaches have accordingly considered the summation of visibles and invisibles – the current account of the balance of payments.

The current account

The first attempts to explain the effect of the balance of payments on the exchange rate were developed between the two World Wars, and centred on the elasticities of different products in different economies. Clearly, if a good was price elastic (i.e. volumes changed substantially in response to price changes) then a balance of payments deficit or surplus will quickly be adjusted back to equilibrium by an adjustment in the exchange rate. If, on the other hand, the good is price inelastic – as we saw in Chapter 1 in the case of oil – the effect of price changes may well be destabilising.

A good deal of work went into attempts to measure different elasticities, but of course as time passes, such things as consumer preference or taste can change quite rapidly, making a nonsense of any empirical work that has gone on before. In the end the arguments were reduced to those of the elasticity optimists, who believed that imports in particular were very sensitive to price changes and who were in the vanguard of those calling for a floating exchange rate system, and those of the elasticity pessimists, who felt there was little or no response to price changes and who therefore argued loud and long that floating exchange rates would in fact lead to greater exchange rate instability.

Empirically there was considerable evidence that the currencies of those countries with balance of trade (or current account) deficits did in fact depreciate, while the currencies of those with surpluses appreciated. Table 2.1 ((a) and (b)) summarises the evidence for the USA, the UK and the Federal Republic of Germany in terms of the current account, and compares these with the exchange rate of the pound and the Deutschmark against the dollar.

Table 2.1 (a)   Current accounts and exchange rates (USA–UK)

(a) Current accounts $ million			(b) Exchange rates	
	United States	United Kingdom	United States dollar/pound sterling	United States dollar/pound sterling (% change)
1978 1	−8.88	−0.46	1.88	5.98
2	−5.21	1.95	1.95	4.09
1979 1	1.13	−2.21	2.04	4.60
2	−1.61	0.54	2.19	7.18
1980 1	−2.55	−0.93	2.39	8.97
2	3.03	8.69	2.38	0.38
1981 1	4.77	10.03	2.19	−7.85
2	1.52	5.02	1.86	−15.30
1982 1	3.56	2.78	1.81	−2.47
2	−11.59	6.50	1.68	−6.95
1983 1	−12.38	1.15	1.54	−8.53
2	−34.29	3.57	1.49	−3.50
1984 1	−46.52	−0.11	1.41	−4.97
2	−60.57	2.05	1.25	−11.23
1985 1	−54.05	0.49	1.18	−5.65
2	−62.38	4.15	1.39	17.79
1986 1	−63.63	0.67	1.47	5.58
2	−75.21	−0.56	1.45	−1.08
1987 1	−74.84	−0.08	1.59	9.12
2	−79.11	−2.57	1.68	5.90
1988 1	−70.28	−10.47	1.82	7.95

Table 2.1 (b) Current accounts and exchange rates (USA–Federal Republic of Germany)

(a) Current accounts $ million			(b) Exchange rates	
	United States	Federal Republic of Germany	Deutschmark/ United States dollar	Deutschmark/ United States dollar (% change)
1978 1	−8.88	4.15	2.07	−8.38
2	−5.21	4.89	1.94	−6.50
1979 1	1.13	0.39	1.87	−3.52
2	−1.61	−6.52	1.79	−4.48
1980 1	−2.55	−6.60	1.79	0.06
2	3.03	−9.34	1.84	2.85
1981 1	4.77	−6.52	2.18	18.35
2	1.52	0.79	2.33	7.24
1982 1	3.56	0.62	2.36	0.98
2	−11.59	2.60	2.49	5.46
1983 1	−12.38	3.56	2.44	−1.81
2	−34.29	0.66	2.66	8.75
1984 1	−46.52	2.69	2.70	1.73
2	−60.57	5.51	2.98	10.35
1985 1	−54.05	5.88	3.17	6.23
2	−62.38	11.14	2.71	−14.38
1986 1	−63.63	16.05	2.29	−15.46
2	−75.21	23.70	2.04	−10.84
1987 1	−74.84	22.04	1.82	−10.99
2	−79.11	23.19	1.77	−2.74
1988 1	−70.28	23.77	1.69	−4.51

In general the relationship shown works quite well, with USA and UK deficits depreciating against the surplus of the FRG. There is a change in the UK experience, brought about by the advent of North Sea oil, but then despite showing record current account surpluses, sterling depreciates sharply against the dollar, as does the Deutschmark, with the FRG also running surpluses.

Something was obviously wrong, and the explanation was that capital flows were swamping the effect of the current account – or, at least, so it seemed at the time. Theories had already been put forward which added in the effect of the balance of payments capital account, and it is to these that we now turn.

The overall balance of payments

If there is no central bank intervention in the foreign exchange markets, then the current account deficit or surplus must be exactly matched with the capital account deficit or surplus because, overall, the balance of payments must balance. This does not apply where central bank intervention occurs in that if a central bank intervenes to support its currency (i.e. by buying it), then there will be an overall deficit in the balance of payments. If, on the other hand, intervention is aimed at stopping the currency rising (by selling the domestic currency) there will be an overall surplus in the balance of payments.

As we live in a floating exchange rate world – for the major currencies at least – apart from bouts of central bank intervention which only occur for a short period of time, there is every likelihood that, for most of the time, there will be a fairly close balance between the current account and the capital account. Thus it may seem totally irrelevant to worry about the overall balance on the balance of payments because one know what it must be. (Over the last three years or so this has broken down at times when there has been concerted, heavy and sustained intervention by central banks attempting to prevent exchange rates moving too far in one direction. However, in general terms the point is still valid.)

In the case of foreign exchange rates, although there must be a balance, the price at which these capital transactions take place is far from known. Indeed, it is the ease with which a current account deficit can be financed (with a capital account surplus) that will determine exactly how far the exchange rate will have to fall, and vice-versa when the current account is in surplus.

The capital account is thus of considerable importance. If it is possible to determine the factors that influence investors' decisions regarding international transactions, then it will be much easier to predict how the exchange rate will move than it would be if the current account balance alone were used. In fact, many would argue that capital account flows are the dominant influence on the exchange rate today, even though the current account was the major factor in the past.

Capital account

The growth of what might be called 'international capital' – that is, money that can be freely invested around the globe – has been very fast indeed over the last 20 years or so. There have been a number of causes with, arguably, the most important being:

1. The increase in current account deficits (and surpluses)

Historically there have always been surplus and deficit countries, but the problem became particularly severe in the 1970s when OPEC quadrupled the price of oil. This led to very large surpluses in the trade accounts of the oil-producing nations, and corresponding deficits in those of the oil-consuming nations.

If the oil-producing countries had recycled these surpluses by investing capital in projects in the deficit nations, then the mechanism would have become self-correcting. However, this did not happen – at least a significant portion of the surpluses was placed in the euro-markets. At the time these markets were pretty well unregulated, but they did perform the useful function of recycling the surpluses to the deficit nations. The problem was that the money was made available by way of loan rather than by direct investment and therefore repayment schedules were not always realistic, and this caused many of the debt-rescheduling problems of the 1980s.

This last point is not the main one at issue here. Rather, the most important point is that the growth in world trade imbalances and the placing of the surpluses in the euro-markets, which are relatively short-term markets, meant that the pool of funds available for short-term speculation grew enormously. Indeed, the size of these funds was now so large that trade flows were overshadowed. Consequently, it was usually the movements of capital – however short-term – that determined short-term movements in exchange rates, and not the changes in trade flows. Of particular importance is the fact that changes in the pattern of trade flows are quite slow moving. After all, many contracts are drawn up some time in advance, and it is obvious that it is advantageous to both buyers and sellers for there to be some stability in business relationships. On the other hand, short-term speculative capital flows gain nothing from loyalty, and maximum advantage can often be gained by moving swiftly from one asset to another.

2. The floating of exchange rates

There seemed very good economic reasons why floating exchange rates should be an improvement on previous attempts to fix exchange rates (for full details see Chapter 7). The use of a market mechanism to take account of the disparities in economic performance between countries seemed obvious. Thus, although floating exchange rates dawned gradually on the world as the result of a failure of the reincarnation of Bretton Woods Agreement – in the form of the Smithsonian Agreement (1971) – there was no sense of despondency in world markets.

Speculative funds will always be attracted to markets when there is a chance of large profits, although this must also indicate the chance of large losses. When exchange rates had been fixed, exchange markets were not attractive as a speculative vehicle, except in those periods when a devaluation or revaluation was imminent.

Floating exchange rates, on the other hand, produced a market where prices could move freely on the basis of supply and demand, and were thus attractive to speculative funds. This did not happen overnight, but grew up as more and more investors and traders realised the attractive possibilities available. As more funds are drawn to the market it is obvious that the role of investment flows must increasingly dwarf the effect of trade flows.

3. The growth of multinational companies

Multinational companies are not a recent phenomenon. Much was written at least 25 years ago on their pernicious or advantageous (depending on one's point of view) presence as a force in world markets. However, they have continued to grow in importance, and their thinking is dominated by comparative advantage rather than by any special attachment to a home base. For example, many US computer companies have moved large portions of their manufacturing process to the Far East because overall production is much cheaper. This type of investment is likely to be based on sound economic judgements and is therefore likely to conform to theories of trade advantage. This type of investment flow could therefore be described as wholly efficient in an economic sense.

Other investment decisions are less dependent on long-term thinking. As exchange rates became more unstable it became important for companies to hedge their exchange rate exposures. Not only could unexpected exchange rate movements lead to losses directly, they might also leave competitors at an advantage. In addition, those who valued companies – for example stock analysts – were impressed by certainty and stability of earnings. Leaving exchange exposures to chance was certainly leaving certainty and stability in the lap of the gods.

Many of the hedging decisions were related to trade flows, for example the buying forward of a currency to purchase imports in the future. These flows, however, are not trade flows as such and to the extent that they lead or lag the actual trade transaction they form an investment decision. Thus although the actual movement of goods is recorded in the balance of payments today, the actual currency transactions may have taken place six or twelve months ago.

The hedging of exposures has moved still further, with many companies taking advantage of the movements in exchange rates to reduce their costs relative to those of their competitors. In fact, there is no difference between this and a speculator making an investment decision, for that is what the company has effectively done. Either way the impact of investment flows relative to trade flows has increased.

4. The increased volatility of interest rates and interest differentials

In the 1970s and 1980s monetarist theories began to assume more importance for the management of western economies. The previous reliance on a Keynesian approach to managing the economy became unfashionable and instead more reliance was placed on controlling the money supply – however that might be defined. One of the most obvious instruments of monetary policy is of course interest rates, i.e. the 'price' of money.

With interest rates becoming established as a means of controlling money supply, the chances of them becoming more volatile must be increased, and indeed this has been the case. In all economies the level of interest rates has been more volatile over the last 15 years than had been the norm since the Second World War. The graph in Fig. 2.1 illustrates the fact with particular reference to the USA and the UK, but similar conclusions could be drawn by looking at any of the free world's major economies. Here there were advantages in moving money from one currency to another to follow high interest rates, provided of course that the expectation was that the currency with the high interest rate would at least hold its value against the currency from which the funds had been converted (allowing for the extra interest received).

The ease with which the money could be moved around was added to by the growth of the euro-markets, including euro-bonds and euro-notes. In addition, the reduction in the effect of exchange controls in many countries, including some in which they were repealed completely, such as the UK, has also added to the speed with which money could be moved from one currency and economy to another.

Capital flows

The combination of the above reasons has led to a massive increase in funds looking for the best rate of return in world markets. It is obvious that an investor will seek to maximise a combination of interest return, and an appreciation of the currency in which he has invested. It should be appreciated that what actually counts is a combination of these two factors and that neither predominates. For example, investors may be quite happy to accept much smaller rates of return by way of interest if the currency into which the investment is made is expected to appreciate substantially. The fall in 1986 and 1987 of the US dollar occurred against a background of higher interest rates in dollars than in either the Deutschmark or the yen.

On the other hand it may still be logical to go for higher interest rates, even if the currency is expected to depreciate – as long as the expected depreciation is modest. This phenomenon occurs frequently within the EMS where it has often been profitable to invest in a 'weak' currency such as the French franc in the period of uncertainty before a realignment, because of the very high interest rates that have been used to support the currency.

If we look first of all at interest rates, we will see that their effects on exchange rates can be divided into three groups, although many might argue that the first two are virtually synonomous. However, the distinction may be useful in explaining the difference in the way the decisions are reached:

1. If an interest rate is higher in one currency than in another, then, all other things being equal, the rational investor will move his money to the high

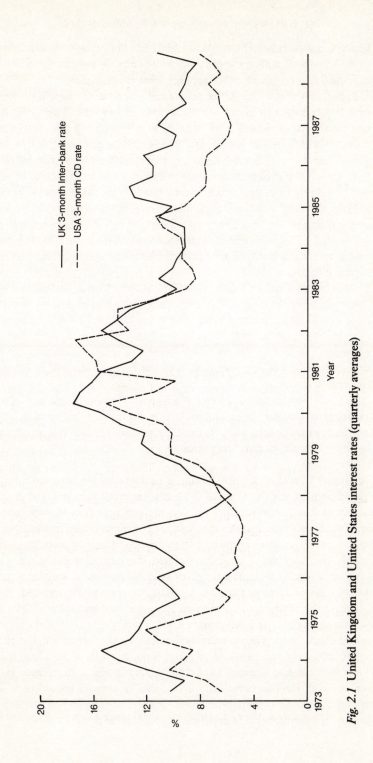

Fig. 2.1 United Kingdom and United States interest rates (quarterly averages)

interest rate currency. Thus we would expect high relative interest rates to be associated with an appreciating currency, as long as the investor expects the currency to either appreciate or at least stabilise.

2. If a speculator has decided that a currency is likely to rise he will go 'long' of that currency, and 'short' of the currency he has sold. Whether or not he uses the forward market it is synonymous with having a deposit in the currency which he has bought and a loan in the currency which he has sold. Therefore, if he has bought a currency with a higher interest rate, then even if the exchange rate does not improve as he expected, he will still be gaining from the higher interest rate. On the other hand, if he has sold the currency with the higher interest rate, the currency must improve in the direction he has expected for him to break even. These gains or losses may be small in relative terms (compared to the size of exchange rate movements) but they may nevertheless have an important psychological effect.

3. Forward premiums and discounts are equal to (if not determined by) interest rate differentials. Thus a currency with a higher interest rate will be at a discount to a currency with a lower interest rate. Therefore to buy a currency forward when it has a higher interest rate will mean that an advantageous rate compared to the spot rate will be obtained. If the currency bought is at a premium, then the forward rate will be 'worse' than the spot rate.

   In these circumstances the cost of a forward premium could well have a major psychological effect, although clearly if the expectation is that the currency being bought will appreciate significantly, it will still be rational to buy it forward despite the premium.

It is important to realise that the timing of payment for imports and exports may differ significantly from that of the actual export or import of the goods. To the extent that there is a difference, the intervening period will represent a capital flow. An example may make this clearer. If an exporter exports a major project overseas – such as a power station – delivery and payment may take place over several years. The inflows across the current account will also stretch over several years. If the company sells its expected flows of currency forward, the effect on the exchange rate will be compressed, the forward cover representing the company investing in its home currency rather than an overseas company for the intervening period.

From the three groups of the effects of interest rates, given above, it is clear that high interest rates will tend to have a positive effect on a currency. However, high interest rates are also often associated with high inflation rates – after all, high interest rates are part of the monetarist prescription for controlling the money supply and inflation. It seems illogical for an investor to put money in a country that is experiencing high inflation.

This apparent paradox can be explained in two ways:

1. If the investment is short term – which many speculative flows are – inflation is unlikely to be a major factor in the investor's thinking and nominal interest rates rather than real interest rates are likely to impress him more.
2. If high interest rates are seen as a correct response to high inflation, and there is confidence that the authorities will in fact control inflation, then the exchange rate will strengthen.

However, permanently high interest rates do probably arise from persistently high inflation. In such circumstances a country is likely to suffer a loss of both competitiveness and confidence. Against such a background, it is quite likely that high interest rates will be associated with a depreciating currency.

Herein lies the difference: short-term considerations seem likely to mean that high interest rates will make a currency more attractive to short-term flows. However, no matter how attractive the interest rate, these flows are likely to slow down if high interest rates indicate that high inflation is not being remedied. Without new money coming in the currency will suffer from any deterioration in the trade flows, which will be exacerbated by any reversal of capital flows as the currency starts depreciating and expectations of continued depreciation gain ground. In the longer term high interest rates are far less appealing.

Expectation of future exchange rate movements

Apart from interest differentials, the second reason why investors may choose to move their investment from one currency to another is that there is an expectation that the currency will appreciate. In Chapter 5 we will look at the relevance of a rational expectations hypothesis to investors' decisions. However, it does seem reasonable to assume at this point that expectations of future exchange rate movements will take account of factors that we have already examined, such as relative inflation rates, the position of the current account and relative interest rates. There may indeed be other factors involved, such as political factors and economic growth, and in addition, for those who invest for only the briefest period, the expectation may be based on little more than a feeling. Nevertheless, for longer-term investors the economic factors mentioned above are likely to be the dominating influences, and to this extent capital movements will equate to economic fundamentals.

However, we have said that the role of relative interest rates feeds in directly to investors' decisions as well as into their expectations of future exchange rate movements. Consequently, it seems reasonable to assume that capital flows are particularly strongly affected by relative interest rates. Indeed, this ties in with central bank intervention tactics which rely not only on direct intervention, but also on the use of interest rates as a direct weapon.

Summary

This rather long chapter is intended to show that concentration on one part of the balance of payments accounts is not sufficient.

Current account and capital account flows are both important, but at certain times the role of capital account flows seems to become all pervading, and currencies appreciate even though the current account is slipping into deficit – a process which is likely to be exacerbated if the expectation of further exchange rate appreciation becomes widespread. Further out, though, such current account deficits become unsustainable and either the market corrects itself or, as in the case of the Plaza Agreement (1985) when the authorities helped to nudge the dollar down, the market takes its lead from elsewhere.

3

THE ASSET MARKET APPROACH
TO EXCHANGE RATES

Until now we have looked at the value of exchange rates being determined by
the supply of and demand for each of two currencies. Essentially, we have
been examining the interaction of flows – the flow of funds into one currency
out of another. In the case of purchasing power parity the change in flows was
caused by inflation differentials which led to one country's goods becoming
uncompetitive in world markets relative to another country's goods. This in
due course led to the exchange rate falling to equalise the currency flows
attached to this international trade.

In the case of the balance of payments approach the flows were caused
either by trade or capital flows. The foreign exchange markets are, however,
being increasingly dominated by investors and/or speculators, as the impact of
capital flows overpowers the effects of trade and invisible flows. It seems
reasonable that investors will look on currencies as assets, and that their
decisions on whether or not to change their portfolio of currencies will be
based on their expectations of how these currencies (and others that might not
yet be in the portfolio) may perform.

The asset market approach views currencies as the same as any other asset.
The demand for an asset is determined by its expected value in the future, as
seen by the pool of investors. They will seek to hold that quantity of asset or
currency which is consistent with their expectation of the future and with their
attitude and perception of the risks involved. The latter may of course
encourage some diversification away from holding just the one asset that is
expected to perform best, because the risk involved in putting all your bets on
just one asset may be too great. After all, expectations are not facts; only
hindsight turns expectations into certainties.

The asset market approach

The price of an asset is determined by the level at which the market as a whole
will hold the total level of that asset available. This has much to do with
investors' perception as to the expected value of that asset in the future – a

concept we first looked at in the preceding chapter. The buying and selling of an asset will be between those who have become less optimistic about an asset's prospects (the sellers), and those who have become more optimistic (the buyers). Obviously, as the price of an asset rises, investors will inevitably become more sanguine about the long-term prospects for that asset unless something has happened to shift the expectation of the asset's value.

The value of the asset is not influenced by the volume of trade alone. The price can be altered by anything that is seen as improving or reducing the prospects for an asset. Furthermore, if we assume that the flow of information to the market is instantaneous, any information that affects the expectations for an asset will be immediately reflected in the price – there will not be a gradual adjustment as would be normal under an approach that considered changes in flows. The motivation of both buyers and sellers is the same. It is just that they view the future in different ways. However, no rational investor would sell an asset if he expected it to rise in value. (Except for those cases in which he sees an even better return in another asset.)

Exogenous factors can be easily assimilated into the approach. A sudden and unexpected shock may well change expectations and the asset price. The change is likely to be swift, and will reflect investors' changed perceptions. It does not, of course, make the prediction of such events any the easier.

The asset market approach to exchange rates

The underlying thesis is that exchange rates should be viewed as an asset. As we have seen, this means that the price will be that at which investors are prepared to hold all the assets available. Does it seem reasonable to use this approach? There are a number of patterns that should emerge if this is the case. However, there is an underlying supporting factor which is worth commenting on first, i.e. that the foreign exchange markets are increasingly being dominated by investors and/or speculators, as the impact of capital flows overpowers the effects of trade and invisible flows. It seems reasonable that investors will look upon currencies as assets, and that their decisions on whether or not to change their portfolio of currencies will be based on their expectations of how these currencies (and others not yet in their portfolio) are expected to perform. This seems a good start, but what other properties might we expect to see if the foreign exchange market is an asset market rather than a flow market?

First, one would expect exchange rates to move in what is known as a 'random walk'. By this we mean that the next movement in an exchange rate is not guaranteed to be related in any pattern to previous movements. Chartists might disagree, as we shall see later, but the rationale is that all present information is in the present exchange rate, and therefore any new information, which by definition must be random, will lead to a random movement in the exchange rate. Later in the book we will examine whether the assumption that all information is in the present exchange rate is a reasonable one, and whether new information will in fact have a random effect, but for now it is sufficient to note that statistical analysis suggests that exchange rates do in fact follow a random walk (for the statistically minded there is no significant serial correlation in exchange rate movements).

Second, if foreign currencies – which are durable assets – are to be priced in the same way as other assets, then the relative price between two currencies today (the spot exchange rate) should be closely linked to the expected exchange rate in the future (the forward exchange rate). More importantly, if new information comes to light which changes perceptions of the future relative values of the two currencies, then there should be a corresponding shift in the spot value. Later, in Chapter 5 we shall look in more detail at whether the forward rate is the market's expectation of the future exchange rate, but in a sense that is irrelevant to the argument here. We can simplify it by saying that there should be a close correlation between movements in the spot rate and the forward rate.

Statistical analysis points to this being the case, but it is simpler to look at how the forward rate is determined. It is composed of two parts – the spot rate and the forward margin. It is apparent, therefore, that a movement in the spot rate will automatically lead to a movement in the forward rate, and the correlation in the two movements will be exact unless there is a compensating movement in the forward margin. Forward margins are in most cases determined by interest differentials (this is examined more fully in Chapter 10), and there seems no reason to believe that these should necessarily change when the spot exchange rate changes. Thus it is reasonable to conclude that a movement in the spot exchange rate will have a major impact on the forward exchange rate, and that currencies do behave as assets when their price is determined.

Perhaps the most convincing argument for the importance of this theory, however, is that the asset market approach would suggest that exchange rates do not adjust smoothly and that over- and under-shooting is likely to be commonplace. It is worth a separate section.

Why do exchange rates not adjust smoothly to expected equilibria?

As we saw when we examined supply and demand methods of predicting exchange rate movements, the equilibrium values of exchange rates predicted by these theories are based on past economic variables. Thus in purchasing power parity, for example, the equilibrium exchange rate is based on the relative value of the two currencies, changes having been caused by inflation differentials in the past. In the case of a balance of payments approach it is past current and capital flows which suggest the equilibrium level.

There may be some attempt to predict future movement by forecasting inflation rates or current and capital account flows, but the equilibrium position owes much to the past and little to the future. When using these approaches it is difficult to explain why an exchange rate should not be at the equilibrium level, and why it should not adjust towards that equilibrium level smoothly. One is left with such explanations as market imperfections or 'noise', neither of which are measurable or useful.

In an asset market approach, exchange rates are viewed as being determined by expectations of future events – be they economic, political or anything else – that are relevant to the determination of investors' expectations as to how the relative value of the two currencies will move. Consequently, a new piece of information – say a worse-than-expected current account deficit – will have a disproportionate effect on the exchange rate of that currency if it changes expectations for the worse on how the current account will perform in the future. On the other hand, if the next month's current account figures are better than the market's revised expectation, the exchange rate movement may be reversed to the original level. Later, in Chapters 8 and 9, we will examine markets' reactions to changes in expectations.

Given this view on exchange rates it seems highly likely that exchange rate adjustments will not be smooth and that over- and under-shooting is likely to be a feature of the currency markets. An investor does not really need a conception of equilibrium. What he needs is an expectation of the way in which a currency is going to move. Will it strengthen or weaken? Indeed, the stock of assets is so large in relation to the normal or trade flows that a piece of information that causes asset holders to switch assets is almost guaranteed to swamp any other factors and lead to a major movement in the exchange rate.

Is the asset market approach really so different?

The evidence outlined above suggests that exchange rates do have more than a passing acquaintance with an asset market, and ties in with our discussion in the preceding chapter about capital flows increasingly dominating the traditional trade flows.

Two questions now remain:

1. Is the asset market approach really so different from what we have seen before?
2. Does it help us to understand and forecast exchange rate movements?

We will leave the latter point to a separate section, but have we made progress? The significant difference from those of the earlier approaches is that the asset market approach ignores supply and demand and flows, and concentrates on the stock of assets and investors' willingness to hold them, and at what price. It is certainly at variance with traditional purchasing power parity theories, which looked at how inflation differentials caused changes in flows, largely through the mechanism of adjustment to current accounts caused by alterations in the relative demand for exports and imports. These obviously form a part of the change in expectations, but they are by no means the complete answer.

The asset market approach also differs from exchange rate theories based on current account factors, which are only a minor extension to purchasing power parity approaches. However, when the effect of the capital account is added to that of the current account, any distinction becomes much more blurred. Although most approaches to the capital account still emphasise its effect on the exchange rate through flows, it is well-nigh impossible to predict the changes in these flows without considering why investors choose to move from one asset to another.

There is a very close link between these two ideas. The asset market approach has added to understanding in the way it has emphasised that calculation of supply and demand curves for individual assets is not only difficult but probably useless. If investors react rationally and adjust their portfolios to changes in expectations, there is no reason to believe that there will simply be a shift in these supply and demand curves; rather, that completely new curves are needed. Furthermore, the factors that determine supply and demand are themselves likely to be changing fast, not only in the size of their impact, but quite possibly in the direction of their impact. The asset-market approach has also concentrated its analysis away from trade flows, a process that is in line with what has been happening in the foreign exchange markets.

The asset market approach with its view of currencies as assets has undoubtedly been a major contribution, but it is not sensible to think of it as an entirely new approach. Rather, it is one that has developed from the balance of payments approach as the latter increasingly emphasised the importance of the capital account.

Has the asset market approach improved our understanding of the foreign exchange market?

The answer is undoubtedly yes. Most of the remainder of this book, and particularly those sections on the practicalities of the foreign exchange market, will illustrate the relevance of this idea, but also to some extent they are based on the thought that currencies are assets, and that analysis of flows is not helpful generally. This is not to denigrate the importance of earlier theories entirely, because investors may well base their expectations of future currency values, at least in part, on what the earlier theories suggest. What it does mean is that a slavish concentration on one or other of these factors or theories is not appropriate, except as we have seen in the longer term.

If the asset market approach has added to our stock of knowledge of the foreign exchange market has it made any advances in our ability to predict future exchange rate movements?

Can the asset market approach predict future exchange rate movements?

Unfortunately, the answer is probably no. The fact that we believe that exchange rate movements are determined by the investors' willingness to hold the assets is of little help if we do not know what determines their expectations. There are numerous factors that may do so. For example, relative interest rates are likely to have an influence because in the absence of an expectation that exchange rates will move, then rational investors will move their money to the highest interest rate.

Inflation differentials and trade positions are also likely to affect expectations, but then so are political factors, along with a wide range of economic factors. Even more important, it is not certain what weight should be given to all the factors, or whether some should be ignored altogether – perhaps just for the moment.

The asset market approach is unlikely to be able to produce an equation or a model which will in all circumstances produce a correct forecast. Perhaps the most important contribution of the asset market approach is that it explains why such a model is unlikely to be obtainable, and it underlines the fragility of any forecast – however confidently it is made.

4

THE MONETARY APPROACH

As we saw in Chapter 3, the asset market approach to exchange rates helped to explain why currencies do not move smoothly towards the expected equilibrium, and why there is a very real chance of over- or under-shooting. However, it was also apparent that this approach offered little towards an understanding of how the underlying economic and political factors interacted to produce shifts in investors' expectations of the future exchange rate position. The likening of the foreign exchange market to any other asset market emphasises the role of expectations but does little or nothing to define the factors that determine expectations.

One approach to this latter problem is the monetary model which, while agreeing with the proposition that the foreign exchange market is an asset market, goes beyond that to explain how economic factors – specifically, relative money supplies – can cause changes in expectations and hence changes in exchange rates.

Underlying thoughts

The exchange rate is, by definition, the relative price of two currencies or two national forms of money. It would seem sensible, therefore, to expect that the exchange rate would be determined by changes in the supply of and demand for each of the currencies. It is pretty clear that this last statement is a truism, and is very similar to all the other models we have looked at. However, the major difference is that the monetary model focuses on the demand and supply of stocks of assets, rather than on determination of the flows that result from the sale and purchase of assets.

Traditional monetary theory stated that any excess money supply in an economy, while possibly leading to some temporary increase in output, would eventually be absorbed by an increase in prices, as the supply of goods would not be able to mop up the extra supply of money totally. This analysis was conducted on the basis of a closed economy – indeed the work was mainly done in the USA, which closely approximated such an economy in the 1960s.

However, for more open economies, the theory was developed further by the international monetarists. The added dimension here was that the increased supply of goods required to offset the increased supply of money could come from overseas. But this increase in imports would lead to a deterioration in the balance of payments, which would in turn lead to a decline in the exchange rate. A decline in the exchange rate would mean that domestic prices would rise as import prices rose, so that, once again, excess monetary expansion would be absorbed by inflation.

These ideas can, however, be combined with thoughts that money is just another asset, but a further dimension needs to be added, i.e. that the expectations of future exchange rates should play a dominant role in determining the current exchange rate.

The role of expectations in the monetary model

If expectations are to form part of the monetary model, then they must influence the relative demands for holding one currency and selling another. The rational investor will of course invest his money where he sees the greatest return. This will be a combination of the relative rates of interest and, even more importantly, his expectation of where the relative values of the two currencies – the exchange rate – are going.

The rational investor will also be prepared to bid up the price of the currency in which he wishes to invest, in order that he may secure his desired asset. Thus the expectation of where the exchange rate is heading is likely to be closely related to the spot exchange rate, or at the very least it will strongly influence the spot exchange rate.

An example may clarify the above, rather wordy, explanation. If a currency is expected to rise over another by, say, 2 per cent over the next week or so, then it will make sense for an investor to continue investing in the rising currency, even though the exchange rate is moving closer to his expectation. After all, a 2 per cent rise in one week is equivalent to an annual rate of return of over 100 per cent, even if we do not allow for the compounding of the rate. However, it will also be rational for an investor to cease buying the rising currency when it approaches his expectation of the future level. Therefore the expected future value of one currency against another is likely to have – as stated previously – a strong influence on the present level of the exchange rate – the spot rate.

Having accepted that the relative demands for one currency against another are affected by expectations, it becomes much easier to include expectations in a formal model of exchange rate determination, rather than to try to explain it away by discussing the rational or irrational roles of speculators in determining exchange rate movements. Thus, if expectations are crucial to the movement of exchange rates in this type of model, then it is vital that the model explains what determines expectations.

The monetary model and the explanation of expectations

Expectations are normally assumed to be 'rational'. That is to say, the expectation of the future value of an exchange rate will be based on the exchange rate at present and a weighted average of all the variables that are likely to affect the exchange rate. However, as we have seen, the present rate will be closely linked to the expected rate, so rational expectations must also assume that the present rate is based on all known information that will influence the expected value. None of this gets us very far. What we need to know is what will cause a change in expectations. Not only that, we also need to know what effect an extra piece of information will have. Will it strengthen or weaken the value of the currency and by how much?

As we shall see in the second half of the book, the effect of various variables may change over time, and the number of variables that is likely to affect the exchange rate may go up or down. In fact, most monetary models are weak on quantifying the impact of new pieces of information on the exchange rate. This may be inevitable, and in any case it is likely that many changes in exchange rates will be due to unanticipated pieces of information. Rational expectations after all suggest that all known information is contained in the exchange rate, and, by definition, any information that is anticipated is known.

However, while the weakness may be inevitable, it does mean that monetary models cannot forecast exchange rate movements accurately because they admit that many exchange rate movements are by their very nature impossible to predict. That is an important lesson, but is there anything else we can draw out of this approach that will increase our understanding of the theories of exchange rates?

The relative supply of currencies

So far we have examined the relative demand for currencies, but at the beginning of this chapter it was stated that the monetary approach was based on the interaction of both the demand and supply for each currency. It seems obvious that this should be the case, but because the analysis of the demand for assets is somewhat fraught, it may well be easier to concentrate on the supply side. It is one of the major tenets of the monetary approach that the growth of the money supply relative to that in other countries will be a major determinant of the price or exchange rate. This is a straightforward exposition that seems both simple and useful. There are of course problems and it is to these that we now turn.

The first and foremost problem is to define money. This is a difficulty associated with all aspects of monetarism, not just the monetary approach to exchange rates, but it is none the less real for that. Clearly, all we need is that definition which best estimates the supply of money that investors perceive as being the stock of assets they may invest in.

Traditional definitions of the money supply concentrated on the split between narrow and broad money. Simply, narrow money is that used for transaction purposes, while broad money is narrow money plus that money which is partly for investment purposes, but which could quickly be turned into cash for transaction purposes if necessary.

Investors in currencies have, as we have seen, one motive, and that is to invest in a currency where the rate of return from both interest and capital appreciation over a period is greatest with a reasonable amount of risk. In the case of currencies, in recent years the change in currency values has often swamped the effect of interest returns. It is necessary to determine what constitutes these monetary assets. First there are straightforward money market deposits, which are obviously a major factor, be they interest- or non-interest-bearing. Although the former is most likely to dominate (forward exchange rates are of course determined by the difference in interest rates on money market accounts, and can be seen as a substitute for money market loans and deposits), very short-term investment decisions may not even last the minimum 24-hour period when interest becomes payable.

A second category is likely to be government or commercial bonds. As long as there is a ready secondary market, these can be treated as being easily converted into cash, but there may be a capital loss if interest rates have changed. Nevertheless, in practice investors certainly do see bonds as forming part of the stock of assets available.

A third category is that of equity investment. Again there are other risks involved apart from that of currency gains or losses. Equally, however, there is little doubt that the exchange rate forms part of the investment decision. For example, in 1987 and 1988 there was a good deal of British (among other) investment into the USA. Time after time the weakness of the dollar was cited as a reason for the value of the underlying asset being so good.

Fourth and lastly there is another category of direct investment, such as real estate or new plant and machinery overseas. In a multinational company, planning for investment must include the relative cost of the investment versus that in other areas of the world where investment could be made. Consequently, once again the exchange rate must be a major determinant as to where the investment must be made. In 1984 and 1985 when the dollar was soaring against other currencies, many multinational companies looked to diversify their production away from the USA because relative costs were seen as prohibitive. Clearly, these are not monetary assets, but nevertheless it does seem likely that the supply of and demand for them will have the same effect on a currency's price as that of monetary assets.

The above four different categories provide us with the problem. Today's investors are likely to see money and goods as directly interchangeable, not only in terms of spending decisions but also in terms of investment decisions. Most definitions of the money supply concentrate on the money market accounts. Even here the definitions have difficulty keeping up with the changing institutional framework. In very few cases do money supply definitions take into account the value of euro-currency deposits associated with that particular currency. If all euro-currency monies eventually ended up in the domestic market, this would not be important, but there is little evidence to support any idea that they do. Many euro-currencies recycle quite happily outside their apparent domicile, but they still form an asset which is available to investors.

Even more infrequently do money supply definitions take into account the supply of bonds available for investment, and it is almost inconceivable that they would take in equities. The definition of the stock of monetary assets is clearly a problem in that traditional definitions are far too narrow to cover adequately the range of assets that an investor sees as alternatives when making currency-switching decisions. It might even be necessary to include certain non-monetary assets!

However, if we assume that most 'investment' decisions in terms of value are made on the basis of very short time horizons, then it may be reasonable to assume that traditional monetary definitions will be adequate for the task. Nevertheless, this is certainly not the full story and as multinational companies become even more sensitive to the effect of exchange rates on their investment decisions, the level of activity in this sector is likely to be increased, and the adequacy of monetary definitions should be called into question more frequently. The monetary approach must concentrate on these shorter-term investment decisions, and ignore longer-term ones.

Back to the demand for assets

Even though the reasons why investors plump for one currency over another are manifold, it is possible to distinguish one or two factors that could be said to predominate.

1. Relative interest rates

The first is the interest rate or, more specifically, the relative interest rate between the two currencies involved. At the risk of repetition, an investor will base his decision as to which currency to invest in at least partly on the relative interest rate. Thus if he expects no change in the exchange rate, he will place his investment in that currency with the higher interest rate. If all investors think the same, that is that exchange rates will not change, they will all invest in the currency with the higher interest rate. This will have the effect of strengthening the currency with the higher interest rate. The investors will have been wrong in their expectations, but few will complain as the error is in the right direction. This process will continue until expectations take account of the fact that the higher interest rate currency has strengthened too far and can then be expected to fall sufficiently to counteract the interest rate advantage.

Some formulations of the monetary model have stated the forward premium as a separate factor. With the premium or discount being determined by interest differentials it does not seem totally real to split this from interest rates pure and simple. There is some anecdotal evidence that the existence of a premium or discount does influence the decision whether or not to hedge, no matter what the view on exchange rate is. For example, a company may be more prepared to buy a currency forward when there is a discount (i.e. you get 'more for your money'), than when there is a premium (you get 'less for your money'). This has no independent status if your view of future exchange rate movements is based on whether a currency is in premium or discount, but many hedgers merely react to the presence of a premium or a discount, without placing it in the framework of an exchange rate view. This is clearly a partial determinant of exchange rate movements, but its effect on exchange rate movements should not be overstated. In any case the country with the higher relative interest rate will be at an advantage.

Relative interest rates are an important factor in determining exchange rate movements, but which interest rate should be used? Given that the forward exchange market is based on euro-currency differentials (because they are free of any exchange controls or other restrictions), it seems useful to begin there. But which period should be used? Should it be short-term rates or long-term rates? Probably the former because of the short-term nature of most investment decisions. Should it be present interest rates, or the expectation of future interest rates? For those invested in fixed interest instruments such as bonds, interest rate changes are crucial to the value of their asset. Should the prices of bonds therefore be included as a separate variable? Are equity prices another factor?

Once again we are reduced to choosing a proxy for the 'correct' interest rate, if the model is to be at all useful, and the best is probably short-term euro-currency rates. It must be remembered that this is a proxy, and therefore restricts the explanatory and predictive powers of the model.

2. Time trends

Over the years it appears that the popularity of currencies has moved in cycles. Thus if one looks at the period of floating exchange rates, there was a decline in the US dollar and sterling which lasted for most of the 1970s in the case of the dollar, and a rise of the yen, Deutschmark and Swiss franc. Both the dollar and sterling staged major recoveries, which became particularly spectacular in the case of the dollar which rose against the Deutschmark, for example in the early 1980s, to a level almost twice as strong as its low point in 1977–78. Subsequently the pound and, especially, the dollar have fallen back again.

These discrete periods can be partly explained by political and economic factors. The initial euphoria associated with President Reagan may explain the rise in the dollar, and the pronouncements of the central banks of the major nations at the New York Plaza almost certainly speeded up the dollar's fall in 1985. However, this accounts for only part of the explanation which almost certainly contains a plethora of other factors. Once again, however, it may be that this time trend can be used as a proxy for these other factors and will at least explain some of the movements of exchange rates in the past.

Relative money supplies

As we saw previously, there are problems in defining money supply, but an increase in the supply of assets (money supply) will lead to a reduction in the exchange rate if demand remains unaltered, which it is likely to do in the short term. Indeed, the UK experienced faster than average monetary growth at the time of extreme sterling weakness in 1976. But, in the case of the recent fall of the US dollar, monetary growth has been relatively modest and would not have suggested the fall in the dollar we have seen. However, the USA has been running large fiscal and current account deficits, which in the former case have created a large supply of government bonds that arguably should be included in the monetary definitions used as a measure of currency assets, and in the latter case a surfeit of dollars relative to demand for dollar goods and investments. It may be that in this period we are seeing the first signs of a need to extend traditional monetary definitions to account for exchange rate movements, because broad money alternatives are being seen by investors beyond national boundaries, but it is too early yet to be definitive.

The main determinants

If the supply of monetary assets of a currency rises while demand remains the same, then normal supply and demand analysis will predict a fall in that currency's price. As an exchange rate is the price of one currency versus another, then it must be determined by the relative supply of and demand for monetary assets of the two currencies. Thus if the supply of the monetary assets of the first currency goes up by the same rate as that of the second currency, and the demand for each remains the same, the exchange rate will not change.

While many other factors influence the expectations of investors, there do seem to be good and supportable reasons for concentrating on relative interest rates as a proxy for the demand for monetary assets, relative money supply and some form of time trend. There may be definitional and measurement problems in the last factor, but on balance a proxy that explains the past seems discoverable. What is not so clear is whether these determinants are useful in terms of forecasting future movements in exchange rates.

The monetary approach as a forecasting method

If we could estimate the effect of each of the above factors on the exchange rate accurately, and at the same time choose the best definition, then it would be a relatively simple task to use the monetary approach as a forecasting tool. Unfortunately, as we have already seen, the latter is difficult because it is by no means obvious which definition of, for example, the money supply should be used. Furthermore, the definition that has worked so well in the past may not work in the future because of institutional changes or alterations of investors' perceptions of what constitutes the range of alternative investments. In addition, the effect of the time trend has already been examined and found wanting when it came to predicting changes of direction in trend, which are almost certainly the most important of all exchange rate predictions.

Thus the monetary approach is not likely to be the answer to exchange rate forecasting problems, which is not to say that it is useless – far from it. To the extent that it has explained past changes in exchange rates, and by doing this has furthered the knowledge of what affects exchange rates, the monetary approach has widened the scope of thought. There seems little doubt that some form of relative money supply does affect exchange rates. Perhaps most important of all, however, is the fact that the monetary method incorporates the role of relative interest rates, and emphasises the effects of capital account movements. Both of these tie in with practical happenings in the exchange markets since the introduction of floating exchange rates.

5

RATIONAL EXPECTATIONS AND THE FORWARD MARKET

What are rational expectations?

The theory of rational expectations states that investors or speculators will take into account all the available information when deciding whether to buy or sell a particular asset. Thus the price of the asset should fully reflect all available information that could influence expectations of the future.

In the context of the foreign exchange market this means that investors use all the available information when deciding whether to buy one particular currency and sell another one. As we have already seen, such information will be crucial in determining the investor's expectations of where the exchange rate is going. These expectations will determine the maximum price at which the investor is prepared to continue his exchange of assets. In practical terms, if the expectations of an investor are that the US dollar will rise relative to the French franc in the future, then the investor will wish to sell francs and buy dollars. If nothing elses changes this will cause the dollar to rise against the franc. However, if the rise in the dollar does not take the exchange rate to the level that the investor expects it to reach, it is likely that he will continue to buy dollars and sell francs until such time as his expectation is reached or surpassed. The rate that will be relevant to this action is the forward exchange rate for the period of the expectation. Therefore, if rational expectations are a feature of the foreign exchange market, then the forward rate should reflect all known and relevant information that affects investors' expectations.

Many readers will no doubt be of the opinion by now that the above is yet another long-winded way of stating the obvious. However, it is worth examining whether rational expectations hold in the foreign exchange market and, if they do, whether this helps to explain past movements, and hence whether it is useful as an aid in exchange rate forecasting.

What is the forward exchange rate?

Chapter 10 is devoted to the workings of the forward exchange market, but for now it will be enough to say that the forward exchange rate is the rate at which exchange contracts can be made for delivery of one currency versus another for a fixed date in the future, with the rate being determined at the present. Thus if rational expectations are to hold in the foreign exchange market, the forward rate should be the market's expectation of where the rate is going to be in the future. Does it seem reasonable to assume this?

The forward rate is made up of two parts: the present spot rate plus (a discount) or minus (a premium) a margin. Chapter 10 will explain in more detail how the margin is calculated, but for now we can assume that it represents interest differentials between the two currencies involved. It seems unlikely, then, that the forward margin reflects the market's expectation of the future as interest rate movements are likely to be independently set, and there is little reason to believe that they should be related to expectations about exchange rate movements in every case.

However, this does not mean that rational expectations can have no part to play. If rational expectations are evident in the setting of the spot rate, then they will also be part of the setting of the forward rate. This will be especially true if the forward margin does not depend on market expectations, because in that case the spot and forward rates will move in parallel whenever expectations about future movements change.

Does the forward rate contain a risk premium?

It might be argued that investors as a group would demand some form of premium when accepting a forward position in a currency. Consequently, there would be an inbuilt bias in the forward rate. In other markets this is frequently true. For example, in the area of interest rates, theory and practice suggest that as the term of the interest rate grows, so the interest rate rises. In other words the yield curve is positive as investors require a higher rate of return for loss of liquidity and increased risk. (The yield curve may of course slope downwards if expectations of a general fall in interest rates outweigh this 'risk premium', but the risk premium will still apply.)

However, this situation cannot exist in the foreign exchange market because the exchange rate is the price for exchanging one currency for another. Thus a positive forward position must imply a negative forward position in another currency. So which way would the rate be biased? Would it be in favour of the currency bought or the currency sold? The other party to the transaction will obviously have the reverse forward position. There is no reason in theory why one or other of these parties should consistently accept one position as inherently more risky than the other. (We assume here that both parties to the transaction are equally willing to hold their respective positions. If this is not the case, then the one who is unhappy will seek to undertake the reverse deal as soon as possible. There is no reason to believe that such a shift will affect the forward rate more than the spot rate.)

In practice there is a risk attached to taking any dealing position, and market makers or price givers will generally quote a spread between their buying and selling rates. As forward rates go further into the future, so spreads tend to widen. They are not biased in one direction or another, except in response to supply and demand. The main reason for the widening is the lack of liquidity in the more distant time periods, and hence a greater risk in accepting a position that may not be easy to reverse with another party in the market.

Could rational expectations be a reasonable assumption in describing the fixing of the spot rate?

The argument so far has been that the forward margin does not really reflect expectations, but, rather, is much more related to interest differentials. However, the spot rate is a component of the forward rate and thus if rational expectations are a feature in fixing the spot rate, they will also be a feature in fixing the forward rate. The question is whether it is reasonable to assume that the spot rate contains all known information that will influence expectations about future exchange rate movements. If we take as our starting point the asset market approach outlined in Chapter 3, this becomes somewhat clearer.

It will be recalled that the asset market approach states that the exchange rate will be set at the level or price at which investors are prepared to hold the stock of assets or currency. It is clear that this level will have more than a passing relationship with the investors' expectations of where the rate is going. Investors will be prepared to buy the currency at any level up to their expectation of where they see it going – with an allowance for interest rate differentials on the currency they buy and sell. There is thus no doubt that the spot rate will be based on the investors' expectations of where the rate is going. The only question now remaining to be answered is whether this expectation will be based on all information known to the investor.

It is difficult to conceive that there could be any possible alternative to the statement made above. There is nothing in any theory to suggest that an investor will gain by failing to take into account all known information, which is not the same thing as saying that all information is known to the investor; and therein lies the problem for the investor and for the forecaster. Both investors and forecasters would find life very simple if they knew and could interpret all known information correctly. However, there seems little doubt that rational expectations do hold in setting the spot rate, and thus the forward rate. Rational expectations pass no judgement on the accuracy of the expectations. Indeed, the forward margin may now be explained within the context of rational expectations. In the preceding paragraph it was stated that investors would buy a currency at any price up to their expectation of where it would reach or peak. There was a qualification (at that point unexplained) that this process would have to allow for interest differentials between the two currencies involved.

If an investor expects the US dollar to appreciate against the yen, from its present level of 125 yen to 130 yen in the course of the next month, he will be prepared to pay up to just under 130 yen for his dollars as long as the interest rates on the two currencies are the same. (It is assumed that deals are struck at spot value and funds deposited in the relevant money market.) If dollar interest rates are lower than yen interest rates, then by buying dollars and selling yen, our investor will forgo some yield. It will not be sensible, then, for the investor to bid up to 130 yen, but to a level which is consistent with the fact that he will receive a reduced interest flow. Conversely, if dollar interest rates are higher than yen interest rates, he will be prepared to pay more than 130 yen to allow for the fact that his yield will be raised.

Forward margins are equivalent to interest rate differentials, and therefore represent the adjustment to the spot rate for this loss or gain in yield. Thus the spot rate is the market's expectation of where the rate is going over a particular period, with an allowance for the difference in interest rates.

Covered interest arbitrage and the forward market

One of the preconditions of forward exchange market efficiency is that there must be no chance of making a guaranteed profit, or even the opportunity of one. This is a very reasonable assumption in practice. After all while it is perfectly rational to take opportunities to make a guaranteed profit, such a profit must mean that somebody somewhere is taking a guaranteed loss. This is certainly irrational and unlikely in a market as efficient as the foreign exchange market. For this reason it is assumed that covered interest arbitrage is a feature of the forward exchange market. In this model it is assumed that the world is divided into two groups of people: arbitragers or hedgers who seek to take advantage of international interest rate differentials, but without accepting the risk of exchange loss, and speculators or traders who hope that by taking a position in a currency they will make a profit when that currency goes up.

In the case of the hedger he will switch funds from a low interest currency to a high interest currency, but will cover the reverse exchange transaction in the forward market to obviate the risk of exchange loss. Thus if the cost of forward cover (the forward margin) is less than the interest rate differential he will make a profit, and conversely he will make a loss if the forward margin costs more than the interest rate gain.

The speculator, on the other hand, takes a position in a currency because he expects that currency to rise over the next time period. He takes his position in the forward market not to take advantage of interest differentials but, rather, to take advantage of currency movements. However, in the last section we saw that the speculator will be influenced by interest rate differentials in as much as he will only bid up the price of a currency to a level which takes account of any interest rate loss.

The interaction between these two sets of players ensures that there is a relationship between forward rates and the expected spot rate in the future, and between interest differentials and the forward margin. Hence the forward rate depends on the spot rate, expectations of the future, and interest rate differentials. In Chapter 10 we will argue that the interest rates are generally set by governments, and hence the influence is from the interest rates to the forward rates and not vice versa. But it is important to realise that this reflects the actuality of the present day and does not invalidate the theory that the reverse relationship could hold.

Most attempts to explain the role of speculators and arbitragers have taken the forward rate as being one rate. From the preceding analysis there does seem to be merit in splitting the forward rate into its constituent parts: the spot rate and the forward margin. If this is done, it is quite easy to explain the role of the arbitrager by way of the forward margin only. Because he conducts a pair of transactions in opposite directions at the same time, he is not interested in the spot rate because this is common to both deals. He is, however, intimately concerned with the cost or benefit of forward cover because this will directly affect his gain in yield by switching from one currency to another. The speculator, on the other hand, is much more concerned with the spot rate, and his expectation of where the rate is going is really the main factor behind his decision. He sees the forward margin merely as a cost or benefit of taking his speculative position. Therefore, in the context of the forward exchange rate, it is the speculator who sets the spot rate, and the arbitrager who sets the forward margin, but the forward rate is set by both of them acting together.

The forward rate as a predictor of future spot rate movements

If we adopt the rational expectations approach, then we must accept that investors base their decisions on all the information known to them, and will always invest in currencies that they expect will strengthen, or at least that they do not expect will weaken. Therefore at the time an investor makes the decision to exchange one currency for another, he must believe that the forward rate is no higher than he expects it to go, and hopefully is lower. However, if all investors think the same, the exchange rate will be bid up to a level that is only just below the forecast rate, allowing for interest differentials. Thus at the time the deal is struck, the forward rate must be more or less in line with investors' predictions of where the spot rate will be in the future. In this sense the forward rate is the market's expectation of where the exchange rate is going. This is not the same thing as saying that the forward rate is a good predictor of where the exchange rate will be in the future. The market's prediction is based on all information known to it at that time, and any new information that becomes available may very well alter this expectation. If the expectation alters, then so will the exchange rate. It will still be the market's prediction of where the future rate will be, but it may be a very different prediction than that at the instant before the new information became known.

The corollary to this is that the forward rate is as likely to be just as volatile as the spot rate, a suggestion that is strengthened if the view that forward margins are based on independently set interest rates is accepted. As we shall see later, this restatement of what the forward rate is or is not has important implications for the way in which hedgers should view it.

With the benefit of rational expectations are we in any better position to forecast exchange rates?

We are in a better position to understand what has gone on in the past, particularly since exchange rates floated in the early 1970s. The sharp, volatile and apparently irrational movements in exchange rates are more easily explained when expectations are seen as the key in fixing rates.

Unfortunately, it is far less easy to say that rational expectations help when it comes to predicting future exchange rates. We can say that exchange rates will move in line with the market's expectation of where they are going, but we cannot define categorically the factors that determine these expectations. The likelihood is that there is no set pattern of influences and as the book unfolds it will explore how some factors fall in and out of fashion. The past may tell us which factors tend to be most relevant and it makes sense to examine these, but a forecaster needs to be constantly aware of changes in variables, their direction, size, effect and, indeed, the variables themselves.

The whole area of exchange rate forecasting is re-examined in the final chapter of this book, when its uses and abuses are set out. Perhaps rational expectations has provided us with the key to what is wrong with many of the traditional economic approaches to exchange rates. They assume that adjustment processes are smooth and generally in the direction of some equilibrium position. This need not be the case under rational expectations. Exchange rate movements will be determined by the advent of new information and its effect on expectations, and there is no reason to believe that new information will become available in a smooth and predictable way. It is far more likely that its appearance will be random, and hence its effect on exchange rates will also be more or less random.

Part II

EXCHANGE RATE REGIMES

6

THE ADVANTAGES AND DISADVANTAGES OF FIXED AND FLOATING EXCHANGE RATES

In Chapter 7 we examine the change in exchange rate regimes over the last 15 years or so. By the end of the period it seems that the enthusiasm for floating exchange rates has waned, and there are increasing attempts to return to some form of fixed exchange rate system. What needs to be examined now is whether this sudden switch to the notion of fixed exchange rates is justifiable in theoretical terms.

The advantages of fixed exchange rates

1. Certainty

In both theory and practice, fixed exchange rates provide some certainty to those who are obliged to consider exchange rates when making business decisions. Indeed, there can be little doubt that in a perfect world international trade would benefit from exchange rates that were predictable. Anything that reduces certainty must in itself reduce the attraction of exporting and importing. What is true for trading must be just as true for investment decisions. It is difficult enough to evaluate investment decisions without having the added complication of having volatile exchange rates completely upset your earlier analyses.

The recovery of world trade after the Second World War was due to many factors, but undoubtedly the 'crawling peg' exchange rate system set up in the Bretton Woods agreement played no small part.

It is true that uncertainty can, to some extent, be removed by the use of such foreign exchange instruments as, for example, forward exchange deals and foreign currency options. Nevertheless, such techniques are never perfect and must add to costs – either directly or indirectly through added staff time wasted. In any case their effectiveness reduces the further forward one goes, partly because markets become thinner and less liquid, and partly because the decisions that need to be hedged are themselves more uncertain – though they will eventually prove just as real. Therefore a great point in favour of fixed exchange rates is that they are an aid to economic growth and international trade.

2. Discipline

If a country is part of a fixed exchange rate regime, then it loses some of the freedom of action to set economic policies which it would otherwise have. For example, it cannot operate expansionary fiscal and monetary policies indefinitely if all the other members of the currency bloc are operating much tighter policies. Such a deviation of economic policies would eventually lead (and probably sooner rather than later) to such disparities of economic performance (for example, in inflation) as to place unbearable tensions on the existing fixed exchange rate structure. Ultimately this must lead to a realignment of the currencies. A good example of this was the attempt by the socialist government of M. Mitterrand to expand the French economy when it came to power in 1981. Unfortunately, the other members of the EMS were adopting much tighter policies. Eventually the strains became so great within the EMS that there had to be both a realignment of currencies, and France also had to adopt more restrictive economic policies. While this example takes the case of a country which was expanding too quickly, the same argument can be used in reverse, and a country that was adopting too restrictive a policy could (in theory anyway) be forced to adopt more expansionary policies if it were a member of a fixed currency bloc.

The discipline is all very well when the predominant member of the currency bloc is adopting acceptable policies to the other members. Thus for much of the 1980s, Germany's laudable anti-inflation stance was transmitted to the economies of the other EMS currencies by the fixed exchange rate bloc. However, as inflation fell – in Germany it fell almost to zero – such a firm anti-inflationary policy was seen as less important, by France in particular, and the feeling grew that Germany was prepared to sacrifice growth for low inflation almost at any price. However, while Germany remains the dominant member of the EMS, there is little the others can do apart from negotiate or leave.

The advantages of floating exchange rates

1. Reduced foreign exchange reserves

One of the obvious disadvantages of fixed exchange rates is that the central banks of the countries involved must intervene on the foreign exchange markets to support either their own currency or that of one of the other members of the bloc, if there are market forces trying to break up the present rate structure. Consequently, there is a need for sufficient reserves to match the cash available to speculators. There was a time when the amount of speculative funds was relatively small, and intervention was manageable. With the advent of trade imbalances around the world, the supply of such funds has increased manifold, and consequently the supply of reserves required to intervene successfully has had to grow commensurately. In addition, intervention will lead to losses in reserves if it is unsuccessful in the longer run. For example, the central banks that intervened in 1987, and, to a lesser extent in 1988, to support the US dollar to prevent it falling too far 'lost' money on the dollars they bought to support the US currency because the dollar continued to fall below the first intervention levels at which the dollars had been acquired.

If exchange rates are floating, then market forces will determine the equilibrium level at which supply and demand will match. Therefore, provided one is prepared to accept the necessary movement in exchange rates, and believe that the market will act rationally, there will be no intervention, and consequently an enormous reduction in the level of foreign exchange reserves required by any central bank in the fixed exchange rate system.

2. Freedom of action

As we saw in the last section, under floating exchange rates there is no need to do anything as long as one is prepared to accept the verdict of the market. Thus a government can pursue any economic policy it wishes. There is no sanction preventing it from doing so, only the change in the exchange rate that might occur. For example, if the French socialist government had not been a member of the EMS, then in theory it could have gone on pursuing its expansionary economic policies and allowing the exchange rate to take the strain.

There is an argument that under fixed exchange rates only the deficit countries have to alter their policies – there being a political stigma attached to a fast-falling exchange rate. Under fixed exchange rates the only way of relieving the pressure is to deflate the economy of these deficit countries, and reduce the overall growth rate of all member countries to the lowest common denominator of the country with the tightest economic policies.

Under floating exchange rates any government is left with the choice of adjusting the position by means of deflationary policies or by way of currency devaluation. The requirement to give such choices makes it very difficult for countries to accept the apparent loss of sovereignty that goes with being a member of a fixed exchange rate system. As is so often the case, countries find it difficult to give up economic flexibility if the lack of this flexibility is seen as economic, or especially political, weakness.

3. Floating exchange rates always find the 'right' level

It is quite clear that the exchange rate at any one time is the rate at which supply equals demand. Thus if we could prove that supply would always equal demand at the price which was commensurate with the underlying factors, then we could say that market forces would indeed push exchange rates to the 'right' level.

This was the view taken by many economists when the Bretton Woods Agreement was in its final throes. It was felt that attempts to fix exchange rates had led to even further distortions in the exchange rate values, and that allowing market forces a free reign would, over a period of time, lead to exchange rates approximating to the underlying economic forces. Indeed, such changes in exchange rates would act as an excellent indicator to governments that all was not well with their economic policy. This theory has a delightful simplicity about it and was certainly worth a try when it became clear that fixed exchange rates were no longer viable because of economic differentials. However, as we have seen in preceding chapters, there is no unequivocal theory to explain exchange rate movements. Indeed, asset market approaches emphasise the likelihood of shocks to the exchange rate system brought about by new information. Such shocks must be random because they are based on new information, which by definition must be unexpected. This makes the situation much more complex and, as we shall see in later chapters, theories have tended to go in and out of fashion over the intervening years. Consequently, markets have shifted their ground several times in terms of what they focus on.

Additional problems are caused because the relationship between economic fundamentals and the exchange rate is two-way. That is to say, it is difficult to determine to what extent exchange rate changes have been caused by movements in the economic fundamentals, and to what extent exchange rate changes have in fact caused them. Such reverse causality can lead to over-shooting of the necessary adjustment, even when viewed in retrospect and set against the underlying economic fundamentals.

The main objection to the simple approach is that it understates the role of speculation in the foreign exchange market. Most theorists believe that speculation will speed up the process of adjustment. However, we shall see in the later chapters that speculation may have nothing to do with economics, and in that sense can be described as totally irrational. It must be dangerous to rely on such forces to adjust the situation, even in the long run, and the reverse causality mentioned earlier may even make the speculative changes at least partially self-fulfilling.

The role of central bank intervention

In truly floating exchange rate systems there is no role for central bank intervention. There are, however, very few cases where totally clean floating has been the order of the day for any significant length of time. Perhaps one of the best examples was in the early days of the Reagan administration, say 1981 to 1984, when the US authorities viewed exchange rate intervention as an anathema.

More common than totally clean floating is dirty floating, where although the currency is not officially fixed to anything, the authorities see it as desirable to intervene now and again. This may be either to stabilise very short-term movements (what central banks would probably describe as market silliness) or, more fundamentally, when a currency's position is seen as deviating too far from what the authorities believe to be some sort of equilibrium position. In either case intervention should be both effective and cheap in the sense that there should be as little intervention as possible. What, then, can justify the effectiveness of intervention?

The first and most obvious advantage is that intervention is much more useful to a central bank when it is seeking to prolong a trend rather than to reverse one. Thus, for example, the Plaza agreement (1985) was so spectacularly successful because the US dollar was already falling, and central bank prognostications and action merely reinforced the trend. On the other hand, the attempt to stabilise the dollar (or at least to stop it falling) at the Louvre agreement (1987) found it much more difficult to influence the market – if it succeeded at all.

Second, intervention needs to be well publicised. As in marketing any other product, the better the advertising, the better the result. There was a time in the mid-1980s when the US authorities preferred to intervene discreetly – rarely admitting that they were in fact involved. On the other hand the Bundesbank and the Bank of England have always been more keen to publicise their intervention. After all if you can get others to follow you, then the amount of intervention needed by the central bank is correspondingly reduced.

Third, intervention is most effective when it is unexpected. One of the disadvantages of fixed exchange rates is that the market expects intervention at predetermined points and knows that it is relatively safe up to these points. If, on the other hand, intervention is unpredictable, then the market will always have one eye over its shoulder, lest now should be the moment chosen for intervention. While the market loves volatility, it dislikes uncertainty. Nothing pleases a speculator more than certain volatility. The most effective intervention is, therefore, that which prevents the build-up of certain volatility. An excellent example of this point was sterling's performance in the spring of 1985. The Chancellor of the Exchequer, Mr Lawson, announced that the falling pound would be allowed to find its own level. This was seen by the market as a free hand to sell sterling. However, as the pound approached parity against the dollar, the government clearly felt that enough was enough, and pushed interest rates up by 2 per cent. While this caught some speculative sellers of sterling unawares, they soon reversed the position, because the government's action was seen as a clear signal that now the market could buy the pound with impunity, and the pound consequently surged up. Here was a clear case of the market seeing certain volatility in two directions – a wonderful way of making money!

One final word on intervention. Traditionally it is thought of as the buying and selling of currencies, but, increasingly, central banks have found it more expedient to use interest rates – to raise them to support a currency, and to lower them to take off upward pressure. Interest rates seem to be a quicker – if somewhat blunt – instrument, but their success depends on capital flows reacting to increased and decreased rates of return, another illustration of the importance of capital flows in setting exchange rates.

Conclusion

The advantages and disadvantages of each system are not clearcut, and even if floating exchange rates appear to be a very 'hit and miss' affair, and even if there are inadequacies in the way floating exchange rates work, they may still be a better alternative to a fixed exchange rate system that relies on governments being better judges of what is required and, even more problematic, insists on them agreeing about what the correct exchange rates should be.

Until now it certainly seems that the burden of adjustment falls much more heavily on those countries with weak currencies than it does on those with strong currencies. During the 1970s and early 1980s that may well have been appropriate when inflation was the greatest problem facing the world's economy. It may not be an appropriate response if the greatest concern were that of recession.

The simple answer is that no system is inherently better than another. The fixed exchange rate system requires an even-handedness and an agreement of objectives that is rarely – if ever – found between the major economies. On the other hand, floating exchange rates create instability, discourage international trade and may even perpetuate distortions. In the immediate future it looks very likely that the world will have to continue to experiment.

7

THE HISTORY OF
THE FOREIGN EXCHANGE MARKET
SINCE BRETTON WOODS

Introduction

At the beginning of the present century, the major currencies were linked to the Gold Standard, which meant that the currencies had a fixed exchange rate against gold, and consequently against all the other currencies with a fixed exchange rate against gold. As the issue of bank notes was linked to the amount of gold that a country held, then any deficit in the balance of payments would lead to an outflow of gold and hence a reduction in the money supply. This reduction would tend to cause a contraction in the economy and a consequent reduction in imports, and to this extent was a self-correcting mechanism.

The development of the world's financial systems, the turbulent nature of the world economy, and a growing tendency towards protectionist policies all led to a growing disenchantment with the efficacy of the Gold Standard, especially as the self-correcting nature of the policy significantly reduced each government's autonomy in directing its economy as it chose. Numerous countries temporarily or permanently broke away from the Gold Standard.

The Second World War spawned many ideas that were intended to head off future conflicts, a reappraisal of the world's financial system being one of them. To this end in 1944 a conference took place at Bretton Woods, which, among other developments, led to the International Monetary Fund (IMF), the World Bank and, what really concerns us here, the establishment of a fixed exchange rate system for the world's currencies, which did have rather more flexibility than the politically, if not economically, discredited Gold Standard.

The Bretton Woods Agreement

Strictly, the Bretton Woods Agreement was not a fixed system but, rather, a crawling peg arrangement. What this meant in practical terms was that the central bank of each country was obliged to keep its currency within a narrow range against the chosen denominator – the US dollar. The actual range was

1 per cent either side of the parity exchange rate. However, if it became clear that the economic fundamentals, and purchasing power parity in particular, had gone too far out of line, then the currency would be allowed a once-and-for-all devaluation or revaluation against the dollar; although it was assumed that this would be a rare occurrence, and was only allowed after discussions with the IMF, who effectively acted as the policeman of the system.

As time went on and there was a growing disparity in economic fundamentals, the need for devaluations and revaluations became more regular and in many cases larger (see Fig. 7.1 and 7.2). This was partly caused by significant disparity of economic performance between various countries, and partly by the fact that the mechanism of adjustment placed too much of the required change on deficit countries, finding if difficult to force surplus nations into the necessary revaluations and realignments.

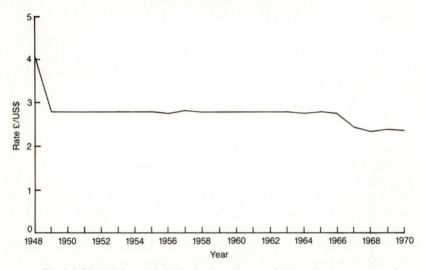

Fig. 7.1 United States dollar/pound sterling, end year value, 1948–70

The problems were exacerbated by the USA running a very large trade deficit, a direct result of its involvement in Vietnam. As the dollar was the denominator against which all currencies were fixed under the Bretton Woods Agreement, this naturally placed the whole system under some strain. In particular the US supply of gold reserves was being depleted.

Continuation of this system became increasingly untenable, and there was a great deal of economic discussion on the merits and demerits of fixed and floating exchange rates. (These arguments were examined in the last chapter.) Thus the first adjustment took the form of a sort of revised Bretton Woods – the so-called Smithsonian Agreement.

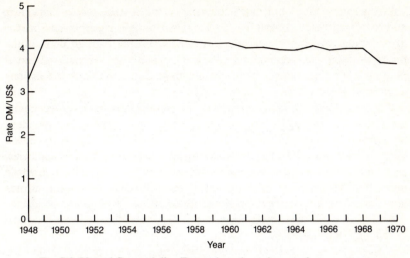

Fig. 7.2 United States dollar/Deutschmark, end year value, 1948–70

The Smithsonian Agreement

This was an attempt to rekindle the earlier glory of the Bretton Woods Agreement. While recognising that parities had moved out of line and needed readjustment, there was no recognition that the system could not hold together in anything other than the short term, unless something was done about the economic imbalances in the major trading countries. The idea behind the adjustment was to devalue the US dollar in particular which was felt to be well overvalued, partly due to inflation and trade deficits engendered by the Vietnam War. This was certainly true and the devaluation of the dollar was desirable, but if economic performance was still going to differ between economies, then exchange rate adjustment was going to have to become a much more regular feature than it had been in the past.

In addition there was a significant change in international cash flows. Whereas in the past, flows had been associated with trade, long-term investment flows or aid, as in US support for Europe under the Marshall Plan, there was a build-up of shorter-term investment flows which were more conscious of short-term economic performances, and much more likely to move on a regular basis to take advantage of what was perceived as a 'best buy'.

The Smithsonian Agreement also broke the link between the US dollar and gold, a link which had been the key to the Bretton Woods system. Once the two were not synonymous it was as if a psychological dam had been broken, and the dollar, once seemingly invincible, was exposed as a much more tenuous thing. However, Smithsonian did not so much collapse as slowly wither away as more and more countries found it necessary to float their currencies as the costs of defending the parity of their currency became too great in terms of both international reserves and the damage done to the domestic economy (see Fig. 7.3, 7.4 and 7.5). And so dawned the age of floating exchange rates which has dominated the scene more or less continuously since then.

The floating exchange rate system

At their inception, floating exchange rates were seen as the answer to the world's economic ills, in the sense that they would automatically – albeit with some time lag – adjust the differences between major economies. It was appreciated that there could well be disadvantages, but on the whole the majority of economists were glad to see the breakdown of the old fixed exchange rate system.

What were not foreseen, however, were the important shocks that the World economic system was about to receive from Middle East realisation that its control of the oil fields all but gave it a monopoly of the world energy market. The massive increase in oil prices that ensued pushed up the world level of inflation (although it should not take the sole blame for increased inflation), reduced world growth and, most significantly for exchange rates, created massive trade imbalances between the oil-producing (OPEC) and the oil-importing countries.

The counterpart to the oil importers' deficits were the surpluses generated by OPEC. These had to be either spent or invested. The relatively small population of many of the Middle East countries meant that spending was impossible to achieve in the short term. Investment flows thus increased, and while some surpluses were invested in the old 'long-term' way, an increasingly large amount was left 'sloshing' about in the world's money markets.

Once an investor is essentially taking short-term investment decisions he must look constantly at short-term factors. Thus the longer-term performance of a currency pales into insignificance when set against what is going to happen in the next month or week. As we shall see later, in Chapters 8 and 9 (and have already touched on in the asset market approach to exchange rate determination in Chapter 3), there is no reason why short-term movements should be towards the long-term economic equilibrium, with the outcome that exchange rates become increasingly volatile. This process was assisted in the late 1970s and early 1980s by the belief in both the USA and the UK that exchange rates should be left to market forces, and that official intervention was both expensive and generally irrelevant. One can argue at length about the merits and de-merits of such a thesis, but it meant that the foreign exchange market had the upper hand, and could drive exchange rates further than might otherwise have been possible. While currency speculators might rejoice,

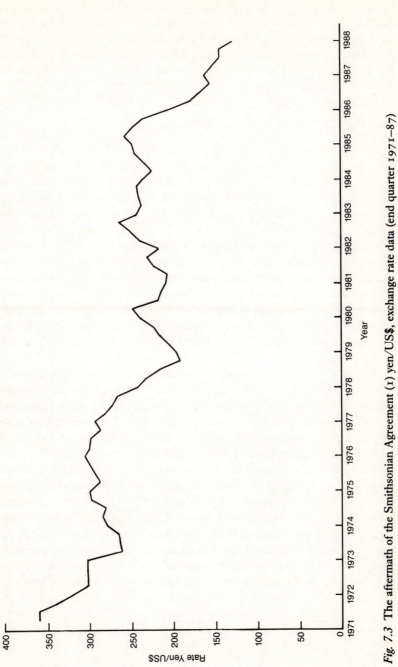

Fig. 7.3 The aftermath of the Smithsonian Agreement (1) yen/US$, exchange rate data (end quarter 1971–87)

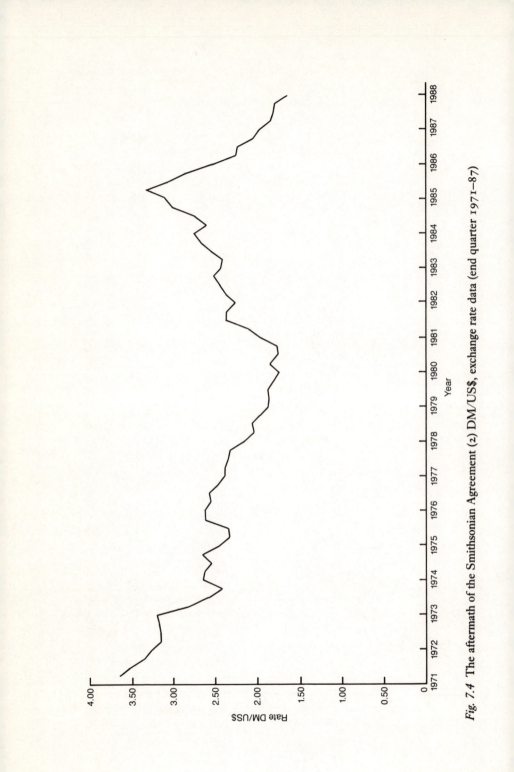

Fig. 7.4 The aftermath of the Smithsonian Agreement (2) DM/US$, exchange rate data (end quarter 1971–87)

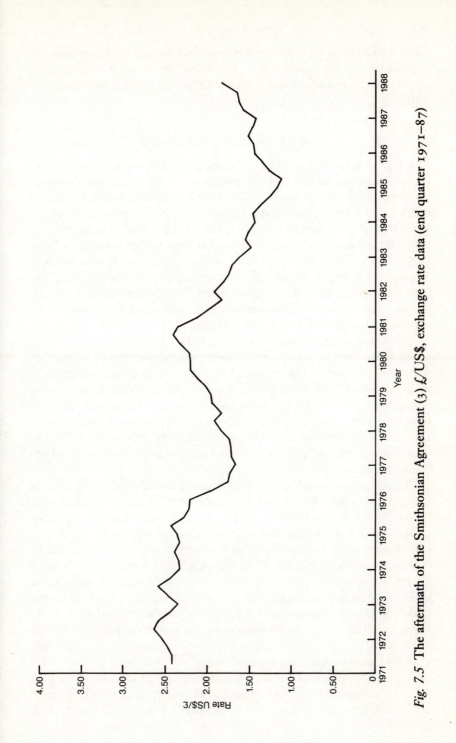

Fig. 7.5 The aftermath of the Smithsonian Agreement (3) £/US$, exchange rate data (end quarter 1971–87)

traders who relied on foreign trade were increasingly under pressure as unpredictable price movements laid their profits to waste. Out of these concerns grew currency blocs, of which I shall look at the most important – the EMS.

The European Monetary System

Almost as soon as floating rates came about, an attempt was made by a number of European countries – mostly members of the European Economic Community (EEC), but also including Norway – to set up a fixed system of exchange rates among themselves. This was colloquially known as 'the snake' and was formed in 1972. In essence it was a fixed system of exchange rates which floated against all the currencies that were not members of the bloc. However, the snake was never really successful, as one by one countries dropped out as they found the task of protecting their fixed parities more and more onerous. In the end it consisted of little more than the Deutschmark, together with one or two currencies that had traditionally been linked to the German currency, such as the Dutch guilder.

However, although the snake was largely judged to be a failure, the concept of linking the currencies of the EEC together stayed alive. It was realised that, without such a concept, full integration of money and monetary policies would be impossible, let alone the drawing together of economic policies. Thus in March 1979, a second attempt – the EMS was set up. Much had been learnt from the earlier troubled existence of the snake, and important improvements had been introduced to make the operation of the system more feasible. Nevertheless, at its inception there were many who predicted that it would go the same way as its predecessor.

The system was joined by all the members of the EEC except the UK. All the currencies were linked to a new composite currency – the European Currency Unit (ECU) – which was a weighted average of all the currencies within the bloc (including the pound sterling). Each of the constituent currencies was allowed to diverge by no more than 2.25 per cent from its central parity rate against the ECU, except for the Italian lira, which had a divergence limit of 6 per cent in either direction (Tables 7.1 and 7.2). In addition, all the members (again including the UK) agreed to pool 20 per cent of their gold and currency reserves so that any necessary intervention could take place. This was triggered when divergence from the ECU central rate had reached 1.75 per cent (in either direction) or when any pair of currencies were diverging by the same amount from their own implied central rates calculated from their ECU values. The advantage of this scheme was that both weak and strong currencies were obliged to intervene, whereas too often in the past it had been the central bank of the weak currency which was left to intervene.

Table 7.1 Currency weights in the European currency units – January 1987

Currency	Weight (%)
Deutschmark	34.93
French franc	18.97
Belgian franc	8.74
Dutch guilder	11.04
Irish punt	1.13
Danish krone	2.79
Italian lire	9.44
Pound sterling	11.87
Greek drachma	0.76
Luxembourg franc	0.33
Total	100

Table 7.2 European currency unit central rates – November 1988

	Currency per European currency unit	Divergence allowed (%)
Deutschmark	2.05853	±1.0981
French franc	6.90403	±1.3674
Dutch guilder	32.31943	±1.5012
Belgian franc	42.4582	±1.5344
Italian lire	1483.58	±4.0752
Danish krone	7.85212	±1.5404
Irish punt	0.768411	±1.6684

The EMS also recognised the fact that because there were disparities in economic performance between the members, it would be necessary to have parity adjustments to redress the imbalances, particularly those caused by inflation differentials. However, at the beginning, partly because inflation differentials were very wide, and partly because the foreign exchange markets did not believe that the scheme would work, realignments were quite numerous (seven in the first four years) and, perhaps even more significantly, were usually forced on the members by the foreign exchange market (see Fig. 7.6 and 7.7). By this I mean that EMS members found themselves resisting market pressures for a period, but subsequently giving in to them and making the necessary realignment.

At this time there had to be doubts as to whether the scheme was viable in this form, and certainly as regards the key Deutschmark–French franc rate, it is doubtful whether stability would have been possible without the French having stringent exchange controls which made it difficult to speculate fully, and also to some extent protected the French economy from some of the worst excesses in interest rate policy which were required to ward off market pressures. However, from March 1983 onwards, the central banks of the

EMS took much more effective control. There was no realignment for almost two years despite several market attempts to catalyse such a situation (see Fig. 7.6 and 7.7). The reasons for the success were, first and foremost, the

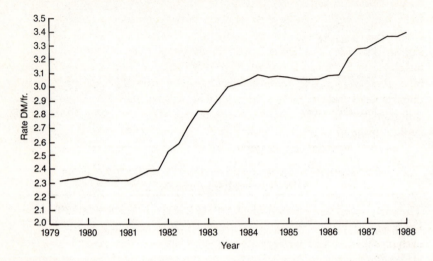

Fig. 7.6 French franc/Deutschmark, exchange rate data (end quarter, 1979–87)

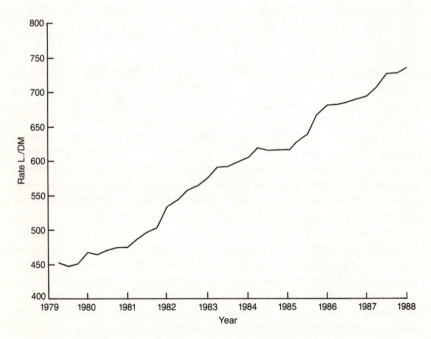

Fig. 7.7 Italian lire/Deutschmark, exchange rate data (end quarter, 1979–87)

convergence of economic performance among the members, especially as regards inflation. If inflation differentials were down to 2–3 per cent, there was far less need for regular and large adjustments in the exchange rates. Realignments do of course still take place, with some countries, for example Italy, finding it difficult to curb inflation in their economies, and with two countries – the UK and Greece (as well as the newer members, Spain and Portugal) still outside the exchange rate mechanism. Nevertheless the EMS has succeeded in that it has reduced the volatility of exchange rates within the bloc, thus encouraging trade between the countries. Perhaps even more important, it is difficult to believe that without the EMS, economic differentials would have narrowed so dramatically. So if it is good for Europe could it be good for the rest of the world?

Attempts to re-impose some stability and reality in the foreign exchange markets

The early 1980s was a period when central banks – in particular those of the USA and the UK – were not convinced that intervention in the foreign exchange markets had anything other than a transitory effect, and could in fact lead to long-term inefficiencies. During this period the US dollar soared, partly due to the attractive level of US interest rates, partly because of better economic prospects in the USA, and partly because the dollar was seen as a safe haven for investors' money. This was a complete reversal of the late 1970s, when almost anything other than the dollar was seen as a safe haven. As the dollar rose still further, US goods became less competitive and the trade deficit began to widen. Despite this the dollar continued to strengthen, peaking against the Deutschmark at around DM3.47. As soon as it had peaked it began to decline reasonably quickly (rather than levelling out as many had predicted) – a process that was speeded up by the Plaza Agreement of 1985, which was made by the finance ministers of the seven major industrialised nations, who publicly stated that they believed the dollar was overvalued, and were prepared to cooperate in intervention to push the currency lower. No second invitation was required, and a combination of intervention and market selling pushed the dollar further down very quickly indeed.

Unfortunately the US trade deficit did not respond in the way economic theory might suggest, and because importers did not put up prices to counteract the falling dollar, but instead reduced what had previously been substantial profit margins, imports were not reduced. In addition domestic demand in the USA remained buoyant, and imports remained high. However, the cost of imports had risen, an extreme example of the J-curve effect, which is a theory that predicts that the trade deficit will get worse initially due to the worsening terms of trade, but will quickly improve as the demand for imports falls, and export goods become more competitive. The dollar continued to fall to a degree that caused concern to Japan and Germany in particular, who saw the risks to their own exporters of an ever-falling dollar.

In an attempt to stabilise exchange rates, the finance ministers established the Louvre Agreement, which obliged participants to hold the dollar's exchange rates within an undisclosed range. The undisclosed nature of the agreement led to much guesswork by the market as to what the ranges should be, but the fall in the dollar was halted and for six or seven months exchange rates stabilised to a degree that had been unprecedented for many years; to such an extent in fact that there was talk of the reimposition of a fixed exchange rate regime, with similar considerations applying to interest rates. However, the authorities new-found confidence soon turned out to be premature – if not mis-placed. A combination of unfortunate and ill-thought-out comments by a number of prominent figures, a collapse in world stock markets, and growing concern about the inaction of the USA to reduce its budget deficit (which was seen as a major cause of the trade deficit) led to another sharp fall in the dollar – in the case of its rate against the Deutschmark and the yen – to all-time lows.

At the time of writing, the question of dollar stability remains a moot point, but it is certain that moves to re-establish fixed exchange rates have been dealt a severe blow. It remains to be seen whether the authorities can establish some form of control and for how long. The question that needs to be asked, however, is 'should they?'. The last chapter considered what economic theory has to say about the advantages and disadvantages of fixed and floating exchange rates. In succeeding chapters we shall examine some of the practical implications of both.

Summary

This has been a very cursory look at the history of the foreign exchange market over the last four decades. We have pointed out two main factors:

1. There have been significant changes in the way exchange rates are treated by both the authorities and the market; and
2. The pace of change is accelerating.

Out of this must come the conclusion that exchange rates and exchange rate systems will remain unpredictable, and therefore dangerous to anyone whose plans include the need to forecast exchange rate movements.

Part III

FOREIGN EXCHANGE MARKETS

8

THE FOREIGN EXCHANGE MARKET

The first five chapters of the book concentrate on the market from economic and theoretical viewpoints, but it is now time to add to these theoretical ideas some practical constraints within which the foreign exchange market operates. While these constraints may not invalidate the economic theories of foreign exchange movements, it is necessary to understand them for two reasons.

1. These factors may have a significant impact on exchange rate movements in the short term – certainly sufficient to make the pattern of exchange rates look unpredictable enough for doubts to be thrown on the underlying theory.

2. A full understanding of the way in which the market works gives one a better idea of what causes temporary aberrations, which at the time can seem more like a change in trend, but which in retrospect prove merely to have been a blip in a totally predicted medium-term exchange rate shift.

This book will not pretend to describe, explain or, least of all, understand all that goes on to make up the foreign exchange market, but it will try to list some of the more important factors. However, one of the risks of writing about the foreign exchange markets is that by the time the book is published some wholly unpredictable factor has graced the scene which tends to dominate market thinking at that time. It is thus important to realise that there is and will always be something unexpected around the corner, and only fools believe that they have the answer to the problems of foreign exchange rate forecasting. Despite all of these qualifications, however, the advantages of knowing how the foreign exchange market works far outweigh the disadvantages of ignorance.

What is the foreign exchange market?

The obvious definition is that it is a market where transactions take place to convert one currency into another. However, such a definition is worse than useless because it does not help one to understand the underlying transactions that lead to the foreign exchange transactions.

Originally, the market grew to facilitate international trade. As more and more goods were traded between countries, the many disadvantages of barter manifested themselves and, consequently, some sort of monetary denominator was required to settle the underlying physical transactions. If there had been one internationally accepted currency, or, better still, if all economies had used the same monetary standard, there would have been no need for the foreign exchange market at all. Indeed, at various times currencies have come close to establishing this role. At the turn of the present century, sterling took the role, and from 1946–71 the US dollar had an even more powerful role to play in international trade. However, for many reasons no currency has been able to sustain its role as an international trade and monetary standard.

Consequently, the need for a foreign exchange market has always been there. What distinguishes the foreign exchange market of today from its predecessors – especially those prior to 1971 – is the pattern of the transactions that underlie foreign exchange trades. At the very beginning, and probably extending through to the 1960s, foreign exchange transactions usually represented the export or import of some specific good or service. Thus if the UK sold more cars to Australia than it bought, then, all other things being equal, there would be a greater demand for pounds sterling than there would be for Australian dollars, and the 'price' or the exchange rate of the pound would tend to rise.

However, with the advent of floating exchange rates, the freeing of exchange controls on capital movements, and the subsequent (though not necessarily consequent) rise in current account deficits and surpluses, there has been a rise in the volume and market share of capital (as opposed to trade) transactions in the foreign exchange market.

There have always been capital transactions, of course, but these usually represented longer-term investment decisions, for example Ford Motor Company's decision to invest in car manufacturing plants in Europe. Now, however, more and more capital transactions are of a much shorter, if not more transient, nature. The next section will go some way to explaining the rise in such transactions, but the overall result has been that the vast majority of foreign exchange transactions now represent these short-term capital decisions. A figure often quoted, though never as yet fully substantiated, is that some 95 per cent of all foreign exchange transactions are of this type. While one might quibble over the exact figures, there is no argument about the approximate scale of the domination of the market by short-term decisions.

The result, of course, has been that the foreign exchange market is now dominated on a trading basis by short-term factors. It is precisely because of this fact that exchange rates oscillate so violently at times, and why the level of exchange rates can look so much at odds with the expected results from economic analysis.

Why is there such concentration on the short term?

The simple answer to this is that most of the operators in the foreign exchange market are there to make short-term profits – they are not paid to take the longer-term view. One of the major reasons for being paid to take short-term profits is of course that it is much easier to measure success or failure in the short term, because if one looks at the longer term, it may be too late to repair the damage when recognition dawns that the wrong course is being followed. To explain this point further it is important to determine the main types of operators in the market.

Corporate dealers

Although companies operate at many levels of sophistication in the foreign exchange market, I will assume for the purposes of this section that we are talking here about companies whose objectives when dealing in the foreign exchange market are to reduce – as far as is possible – the risk posed to the companies by foreign exchange flows in either direction. Such a company will thus be anxious to turn its foreign currency flows into its base currency, using, for example, the spot, forward, futures or foreign currency options market. The crucial point, however, is that each foreign exchange contract will have a matching movement in either a traded good or service. To this extent the transaction is 'real' and will impact on the economy's current account of the balance of payments.

Furthermore, the company may decide to invest or dis-invest abroad. If either of these actions result in a cash flow to or from the parent company's domestic operations, then the need for a foreign exchange transaction will arise. Such a flow of foreign exchange will affect the capital account of the country's balance of payments.

Both the above types of transactions are based on longer-term decisions in the sense that trade transactions do not take place to maximise the return on foreign exchange, but, rather, to maximise the profit to the company from selling or buying its goods abroad. Investment decisions, too, are based on long-term considerations as to whether the investment will be of benefit to the company over the course of a number of years.

While these types of transactions were in the majority, and arguably that was the case when there was a fixed exchange rate regime – say up until the early 1970s – then foreign exchange rate movements were associated with decisions based on longer-term economic and political factors. However, as the importance – in terms of volume – of these decisions waned, so foreign exchange rate movements became increasingly dominated not by trade-related nor major investment decisions, nor even by companies.

Company hedging decisions

If a company is importing goods in a foreign currency from overseas, then it will often seek to protect itself by buying forward the currency it will need in the foreign exchange market. This means that the actual flow of goods will be preceded by a currency transaction, but the overall effect on the foreign exchange market will be neutralised in the end. However, such hedging decisions do create investment flows of a sort, because when the company buys the foreign currency forward, it is in effect investing in that currency until the delivery of the goods. This type of transaction has been going on for years and is thus not really new, except in that the removal or reduction in exchange controls in many countries has made the task somewhat easier and less bureaucratic.

What the removal of exchange controls has also done is to allow companies to adopt a more active hedging policy. It is all very well to establish certainty in one's own business, but if a competitor is able to gain an advantage by adopting a less certain hedging policy, then there is little comfort in being fully hedged if you can no longer sell your product. Thus, although a company may hedge all its foreign exchange transactions completely, it is still at risk if a competitor who does not hedge is able to take advantage of a favourable movement in exchange rates, and so be in a position to sell his goods more cheaply.

Consequently, it has become increasingly prevalent for companies to hedge more actively. They are no longer content to simply cover forward automatically, but to act like any other investor and decide that their expectation of a currency is whether it will go up or that it will go down. As new information comes along, so their expectation may alter, and so may their hedging decision. It may be that the same trade flow will first be hedged, then un-hedged and then perhaps hedged again.

All these decisions are only obliquely related to underlying trade flows, and the actual decision process would be more properly described as an investment decision.

Portfolio investment

Investment has always been an important influence on the foreign exchange markets, but since the mid-1970s there has been a continuing and significant change in the way that investment flows have impacted on exchange rates.

During the period of fixed exchange rates overseas investment still took place, but decisions as to whether or not to invest were based on long-term expectations and economic fundamentals. Consequently, a decision to invest overseas would be based on such factors as expectations of economic growth over the next few years, expectations about inflation over the next few years, the possibility of restrictions being placed on international trade, or a decision could even be based on just wishing to diversify a company away from relying solely on the economy of one country. It is true that expected changes in the value of a country's exchange rate were also taken into account, but by no means was it the overriding consideration.

However, with the advent of floating exchange rates, currency movements became more volatile and the consequences of changes in a currency's value became increasingly important to an investor wanting to place his money outside his own country. All the more fundamental factors still came into play, but there was a shift in their relative importance. The growing importance of exchange rate movements led to two significant changes:

1. There was a shortening of time horizons in investment decisions, as it was the short-term movements in a currency that could so significantly enhance or detract from the performance of an overseas investment.
2. Whereas the main direction of the causal relationship between portfolio investment and exchange rate changes had been the former to the latter, there was an increasing tendency for the causal relationship to be two-way or even reversed, so that exchange rate changes (both actual and expected) became an important if not overriding factor in portfolio investment decisions.

Speculation and the growth of the euro-markets

While it would be unwise to underestimate the importance of either trade or portfolio investment flows in determining exchange rate movements, it would be equally foolish to ignore the more speculative end of the market. Although no accurate statistics are available, most estimates suggest that no more than 10 per cent of transactions are directly associated with trade and portfolio investment flows carried out by corporates. This may underestimate the total number of related flows, in that one 'real' trade transaction may lead to more than one exchange transaction before a balance in the system is reached. Nevertheless, despite these provisos, most dealers would say that an overwhelming proportion of the value of foreign exchange transactions would represent more speculative decisions.

By their very nature, speculative transactions are made on a short-term basis – often a very short-term basis. Indeed, in the foreign exchange market views are adopted for a matter of minutes rather than days. This is not to say that when a dealer takes a decision about buying or selling a currency, he does not believe that the trend he is predictiing will last for more than a transient moment. What he is prepared to do, and what distinguishes him from a portfolio investor, is that he is prepared to reverse his decision very quickly indeed if it turns out to have been the wrong one, or when his initial objective has been achieved.

As we shall see in Chapter 11, the foreign exchange market at the level of the foreign exchange trader is much more akin to game theory than it is to economic theory. Dealers do not always seek to maximise, but, rather, they seek to make profits while reducing risks to an acceptable level. One thing above all governs the actions of participants in this section of the market and that is that they earn their salaries by making a profit. They are not paid on the basis that they should seek to establish exchange rates at some level which equates with some combination of medium-term economic fundamentals. The concentration on short-term factors and immediate profits will often lead to dealers taking decisions that are against these fundamentals. The question is whether such distortions have any significant effect and whether their influence can extend far enough into the future as to change the very fundamentals on which they were meant to be based.

What affects dealers' perceptions of a currency?

Many of the factors that affect dealers' perceptions of a currency are the same as those outlined in the first half of this book. That is to say, the economic variables that theoretically govern exchange rate movements are recognised if not always understood by those who undertake speculative transactions in the foreign exchange market. However, there are other factors also, and indeed in the very short term, even the theoretical influences may have unpredictable effects on the exchange rate of any currency.

The 'normal' economic factors are:

(a) balance of payments – both current and capital account;
(b) relative inflation rates;
(c) relative interest rates;
(d) economic growth;
(e) bond market performance;
(f) equity market performance;
(g) political factors;
(h) official intervention.

In Chapter 9 we will examine some of the apparent inconsistencies that changes in these factors have created in foreign exchange rate movements, but for now it will be sufficient to acknowledge that very often the exchange rate changes not because of the reality of any one of these variables, but, rather, due to the expectation of what it might be. A phrase often heard in newspaper comments about the foreign exchange market is 'the market already discounts the likelihood of . . .'. Roughly translated, this means that the market has already made up its mind about what a particular statistic will be, and therefore will only be disturbed from its equilibrium if the actual outcome is very different from the expected result. Therefore for the short-term market operators the outcome of an economic statistic is much less important than the variance between the actual outcome and the expectation of that outcome.

Theoretically there is nothing wrong with this approach since, for example, the rational expectations approach would expect a market to make forecasts, to adjust the exchange rate in advance, and only to change its actions if there were to be a variance or a change in information. However, the problem is that the speculative end of the market bases its forecasts on very incomplete information, often merely following the forecast of whoever happens to be the fashionable 'guru' of the time.

Again, the adoption of what one might unkindly call a 'pseudo-approach' to the economics of the foreign exchange market leads to the concentration on short-term effects. For example, most operators in the market will look no further than the next round of statistics to be released, but, perhaps even more disturbingly, they will frequently have little conception of the past history of any particular economic series. There is nothing inherently wrong in this because market dealers make their profits by forecasting a currency's movements over a very short time period. It does not matter if this movement is illogical when measured against longer-term factors, as long as it makes money before it is reversed.

What is the overall effect of concentration on the shorter term?

It should be made clear right at the outset that it is very doubtful whether wrong short-term decisions can have any major effect on long-term trends in any currency's movement – especially if these are measured by way of averages. However, it can and does mean that the path towards this long-term trend is a very volatile one. There is no reason why a short-term movement in exchange rates should be towards the long-term trend, as long as participants in the market believe that a move in the opposite direction will make money for them now.

In the past, particularly when fixed exchange rates ruled the roost, many more operators were taking longer-term decisions for investment purposes, and a much higher proportion of foreign exchange deals represented trade transactions. Both these categories acted as a force to push currencies back to their longer-term trend. However, a speculator seeking immediate profit has no interest in pushing a currency gently back to its trend; in fact, quite the opposite. There is nothing the true speculator would love more than enormous volatility as long as the market remains sufficiently liquid for him to deal when he wants to.

As volatility increases, so more and more speculators appear, and more and more companies have to actively hedge their overseas trade decisions. Consequently, the market tends to become more volatile. Fund managers who are essentially taking long-term investment decisions also have to actively hedge their currency positions, not only to reduce the risk of loss should the currency move adversely, but increasingly to make money in order to keep up with the performances of their peer group of fund managers. Put very simply, an increased attention to the short term will lead to increased volatility of exchange rates.

9

THE FOREIGN EXCHANGE MARKET AS A PERFECT MARKET

The 'perfect' market

In an economic sense the foreign exchange market is as close as makes no difference to being a perfect market. That is to say, as indicated by the following, it matches the economic criteria for a perfect market.

1. It has an homogeneous product: that is, no matter from where you buy your dollar, Deutschmark or pound, it is always the same and is freely interchangeable.
2. There are many buyers and sellers: this is certainly true, as the market is made up of an almost immeasurable number of participants – both very large and very small – and every shade in between.
3. Freedom of entry: certainly, anybody can join in the market freely. Costs of entry are low and unless exchange control regulations preclude individuals of any country from participating, there are no market restrictions governing entry.
4. Freedom of information: there is no monopoly of knowledge in the market and insider trading is less important than in any other market. However, this does not necessarily imply equality of information. Good information is expensive and not all market participants have the time or the wherewithal to gather truly up-to-date information. None of this, however, negates the proposition that there is freedom of information in the foreign exchange market.

If a market is perfect in an economic sense, this implies that the price in the market will always be that which equates supply and demand; but only the supply and demand at that moment – economic theory cannot help assist directly when it comes to estimating how supply and demand will change in the next instant. The 'traditional' economic theories work on the adjustment process over the medium term, and even the asset-market-linked approaches, which acknowledge that the change in expectations cause sharp movements in exchange rates, do not in any way suggest that these changes are predictable.

Certainly, common sense would not suggest that a perfect market moves the price towards a long-term equilibrium price, or at least that it does not necessarily do so smoothly. There may be a great deal of volatility in the adjustment process.

How the market reacts to economic and other information

There was a time when it was possible to make money from the foreign exchange market by having early information of economic or political events that had already taken place. Before the Second World War, for example when wireless telegraphy was available, but not widely, and when news reports could take two or three days to each the outside world, if you had some means of knowing with certainty that a particular event had taken place, then it was possible to undertake exchange deals that would be to your benefit when the news became common knowledge.

But those days are of course long gone, and in these days of instantaneous news information, whether it be from national broadcasting institutions, or from one of the press agencies, it is extremely unlikely that anybody can even hope to have anything more than a fleeting opportunity to gain from prior knowledge; which is not to say that every operator in the market will have the same information, but, rather, that any operator will have the opportunity to gain access to the same information. The reason why opportunity and actuality are not one and the same thing is of course cost. Instantaneous information is very expensive. Access to news services is far from cheap, and it is even more expensive when one takes into account that it is necessary to have access to all news services, just in case one service has some vital piece of information as a scoop or exclusive or has published the information a minute or so earlier than the others.

Up-to-date and accurate information is essential if profits are to be generated from the foreign exchange market. Those with better information will, all other things being equal, make more money than those with poorer information. The corollary of this, not surprisingly, is that those with the wherewithal to invest heavily in the technology of foreign exchange have the greater chance of winning. The above has concentrated on how the market gets its information and who gets the best information, but it tells us little of how the market reacts to or uses the information.

One comment is obvious. If the market is spending a considerable amount of money on acquiring speedy information, then it is very likely that the initial reaction to any piece of news will be well-nigh instantaneous. Or to put it another way – not much analysis is going to be possible between the news breaking and the market reacting. Therefore most instantaneous reactions evolve from analysis that has taken place before the news has broken. Typically, this means that a greal deal of time and effort goes into forecasting the next economic release or the outcome of some political meeting. Very often this will be reflected and published as a 'market consensus', which, it is believed, will already have been discounted in the exchange rate. The instantaneous reaction will then be based on the deviation of the actual outcome from the expected outcome, and not on the actual outcome itself.

The approach outlined above relies on two very major assumptions. First that forecasts of the expected news will be accurate, and secondly, and perhaps more important, that the market will have digested this expectation fully and will already have adjusted the exchange rate to take account of this new information in a way that accurately reflects the underlying economic, political and many other factors. A set of assumptions such as this is demanding to say the least, and it seems unlikely that the hypothesis that the market does fully take on board its expectation would stand up to very rigorous testing.

As we saw in Chapter 5 rational expectations rely on the market basing its expectation on all known information, but it does not suggest that the information is accurate, nor that the response to the information is 'economically corect'. Some examples should make this somewhat clearer.

Balance of payments data

Month by month balance of trade and current account figures are very difficult to measure, let alone predict. This is not surprising given the fact that they are made up of the differences between two very large numbers – imports and exports. Thus, even a small percentage error in either of the two components is very likely to lead to a major inaccuracy in the difference. Furthermore, given the seasonal nature of trades such figures need to be seasonally adjusted to be meaningful. Such seasonal adjustment inevitably means a subjective judgement, no matter how well the statistical analysis leading to the seasonal adjustments has been undertaken.

One would think that given these difficulties it would be worthless to try to predict the outcome of one month's figures, and that forecasters should concentrate on the longer term instead, say the annual figures. Yet this is not the case. Each month much time and effort goes into estimating what the figures for that month are going to be. Based on these estimates, however ragged they may be, the market is said to adjust its views on exchange rates, and buy or sell the currency accordingly. This leads to the phrase that the market is already discounting the information. When the actual figures are released, the market will concentrate on whether the outcome is better or worse than the expectation, and will then adjust the rate accordingly.

It would be very surprising indeed if this rather inexact process were in some way to arrive, in the short term, at levels that are commensurate with the long-term position of the trade and current accounts. Therefore, short-term or instantaneous reactions to new economic data do not, and almost cannot, reflect a considered opinion of the longer-term prognostications.

Furthermore, as we have seen in Chapter 2, the current account is not the full story. The capital account is also vital, but unfortunately it is even more difficult to measure, usually only being produced quarterly rather than monthly. Thus the market is never in a position to judge the total balance of payments data accurately until well after the information has any relevance to the foreign exchange rate.

Money supply data

The concentration of the foreign exchange market on money supply data coincided, albeit with something of a lag, with the rise in monetarist policies and the recognition that increases in the money supply were in some way related to future inflationary increases. To that extent at least, the concentration was logical. If governments are basing their future economic, and even political decisions, on increases or decreases in the money supply, then the money supply should be a good predictor of governments' intentions, and therefore a good leading indicator of future economic performance.

So far so good, but governments in several countries, particularly in the UK and the USA, have found the practice of monetarism much more difficult to undertake than the theory would have suggested. Perhaps the most obvious of the difficulties was that of deciding which monetary aggregate most accurately predicted the future rate of inflation. Sophistication in the financial markets has lead to distortions in many money series as monetary product innovation and disintermediation took place. Consequently, we have seen a plethora of monetary aggregates, and, especially in the UK a number of switches in emphasis from one statistic to another.

Not surprisingly the foreign exchange market has followed these fashions. Again it could be argued that it is right to concentrate on the figures that a government is watching, because it is these figures that will determine future policy. Quite true, but it would be wrong to follow that up by suggesting that the foreign exchange market itself believed in some form of monetary theory determining exchange rate movements; the market is merely following political changes to economic policy.

A further major problem occurred, particularly in the USA, relating to the frequency with which monetary data was released. In the USA it is the practice to release the narrowest form of monetary aggregate (M1) on a weekly basis, while the broader aggregates (M2 and M3) are released on a monthly basis, which is the customary frequency in most other developed countries. For several years in the early part of this decade, the Federal Reserve Board (Fed) or the Central Bank of the USA, based its analysis of the monetary conditions on the behaviour of all these aggregates against a set of predetermined targets.

For most of the time the Fed gave more or less equal prominence to all these aggregates, but this was not true of the market. Because M1 was released on a weekly basis, and therefore was attractive to the market purely by virtue of its frequency, the foreign exchange market (and incidentally many of the money markets inside and outside the USA) almost completely convinced itself that M1 was the most important aggregate on which to focus. This led to weekly fluctuations in the exchange rate as M1 vacillated between good and bad. While there were periods when its performance was such as to cause changes in economic policy, for much of the time the volatility of the weekly figures was caused by little more than measurement error and the inadequacies of the seasonal adjustment process. Here indeed was a classic example of the market taking short-term information and extrapolating it into a long-term trend, a trend which next week's figures might reverse.

The two illustrations given above are by no means unique, and almost any regularly reported economic statistic has had its hey-day. The important points to realise are that, first, while the market attaches great importance to economic data, it does not necessarily look upon the releases as a currency economist would. In particular, the market is much more interested in deviations from the expected than it is with what the figures actually mean for the currency in the longer term. Second, the market is apt to follow fashions, some of which do have some relevance in that they do, to some extent at least, reflect the way the government is thinking, but in other cases the link between the statistic and policy is far more tenuous. Furthermore, in some cases the accuracy of the data when first released can be doubtful and subject to later major revisions.

The other factors that make up a perfect market

Most of this chapter has concentrated on the way freedom of information works within the foreign exchange market, and in particular how it is that the information itself, and not so much its quality, has the greater effect on the market's short-term thinking and dealing decisions. This is because the information revolution has made such a great impact on the world's currency markets. However, it is worth spending a few lines on the other criteria which are necessary for a perfect market in economic theory.

1. Many buyers and sellers

As we saw in Chapter 8, in the days of fixed exchange rates most transactions were either trade related or based on long-term investment decisions. With the advent of floating exchange rates and the appearance of major imbalances in countries' external trading positions, the possibility for much shorter investment decisions became more viable. This led initially to more participants in the markets as banks in particular set up larger and larger dealing rooms, both to service their trading and investment customers and also as a source of direct profit from getting currency movements 'right'. Moreover, as time has gone by the volume of money traded on the foreign exchange markets has grown in an almost exponential way, and the number of participants has also grown. Most of these participants, typically those who have trading or long-term investment interests, have accounted for a smaller and smaller share of the total turnover. To a great extent the massive increase in turnover has been concentrated in the hands of banks and other like-minded financial institutions. The numbers of such institutions are too great to constitute anything like an oligopoly situation, especially in those time-zones with the greatest liquidity. Nevertheless, while the concentration of dealing volume probably does not infringe on the criterion necessary for perfect competition, the market is not becoming more differentiated – quite the opposite.

2. An homogeneous product

As was stated earlier, there is little doubt that in the foreign exchange market there is a series of homogeneous products – these are not the actual currencies themselves, but the exchange rates to which they lead. It is self-evident that although the pricing from one foreign exchange market participant may differ slightly from that of another, the products that will be exchanged will be exactly the same.

3. Freedom of entry

In those countries that do not have exchange controls, there is no barrier to participating on the foreign exchange market. Anybody can buy or sell a currency, and it is an activity that most companies will engage in from time to time. This is not to say that everyone will be able to participate equally – much will depend on the resources that any participant is prepared to put into the venture – but, then, this is no different from any other form of economic activity.

Where there are exchange controls, there may indeed be a bar to entry to the foreign exchange market. After all, that is the usual reason for having exchange controls. Such restrictions do not make the foreign exchange market as a whole imperfect, but they do mean that the market in such currencies will not conform to the rules of perfect economic markets.

Conclusion

This chapter has attempted to show that the foreign exchange market is probably the nearest there is to a perfect market, in that it conforms to all the criteria laid down in economic theory, with only a few minor blemishes. However, what this chapter has also tried to show is that such a free market, while always equating supply and demand at the appropriate price, will not necessarily lead to exchange rates converging towards the long-term equilibrium levels that some of the earlier economic theories, explained in the first half of this book, would suggest. In particular, the reaction to short-term economic or political data bears very little relationship to what the economic data is saying about the long term.

The asset market approaches acknowledge this, but make little headway in incorporating this knowledge into forecasting accuracy. Indeed, the speed of the change in expectations overwhelms even the statistical work that has been used to support the theory. Exchange rate changes occur many times a day – even significant changes – and an analysis which concentrates on monthly, or even daily figures, understates the volatility to a major degree. As we shall see in the last chapter of the book, this has important implications as to how economic forecasts of exchange rate movements should and should not be used.

10

THE FORWARD EXCHANGE RATE
MARKET

The spot exchange rate market has distinct limitations when it comes to helping commercial companies to hedge international transactions. Although it allows cash flows in foreign currencies to be converted into the currency required by the commercial organisation, it cannot cope with cash flows that, although known, will not materialise until some time in the future. It was precisely to meet this need that the forward exchange rate markets grew up.

How is the forward exchange rate calculated

As we saw in Chapter 5, the forward rate is simply the spot exchange rate adjusted by a premium or discount. This premium or discount must – in general and in a free market – be determined by the interest rate differential between the two currencies. A simple example will explain why.

Let us assume that a particular investor has $US 1 million. The interest rate for one year's deposit in dollars is 5 per cent, whereas the interest rate for a deposit in sterling is 10 per cent. Clearly, the investor could raise his interest yield by converting the dollars into sterling, and depositing this amount for one year. Equally clearly, he runs the risk that at the end of the year the pound will have depreciated against the dollar by more than the extra interest (i.e. by more than 5 per cent) so that, overall, the investor will have lost when compared with a dollar deposit for one year.

One way out of the dilemma would be to undertake two exchange transactions simultaneously. First the investor would sell dollars and buy sterling for spot value, and then he would contract to sell the pounds for dollars in one year's time. Because both contracts are struck at the same time, the spot rate will be the same in each case, the only difference between the two rates will be the forward premium or discount.

Now if this discount or premium does not more or less equal the difference between the two interest rates in dollars and sterling, it will be possible to make a guaranteed profit or arbitrage by undertaking a risk-free pair of transactions. That is to say, if the forward cover is less than 5 per cent, then if an investor deposits his money in sterling but covers the forward exchange rate at the same time, he will profit from the difference between 5 per cent and the cost of forward cover. If on the other hand, the cost of forward cover is more than 5 per cent then the reverse transaction will be profitable, i.e. borrow sterling, convert it to dollars and deposit it for one year, while converting the exchange risk back into sterling in one year's time by covering forward now. In a perfect market such as the foreign exchange market, such arbitrage opportunities cannot and do not exist for anything other than brief periods. Thus the forward exchange rate is the spot rate adjusted for the interest differential between the two currencies.

Exceptions to this rule

The perfect relationship between interest rate differentials and the forward exchange rate margin only exists where there is a free deposit/loan market in both currencies. Strictly speaking, the interest rate differentials that should be used are those of the euro-currency market because it is through this market that any arbitrage would take place. In most freely traded currencies there would, however, be a close relationship between domestic interest rates and euro-currency interest rates, or else an arbitrage opportunity would exist between these two markets as well (because no currency risk is involved). However, if exchange controls are placed on one or other of the currencies, then the relationship may no longer hold good.

For example in France, particularly just prior to the EMS realignment in March 1983, the government used the forward exchange market to help protect the French franc from adverse speculation. Basically, the authorities (the Bank of France) bought French francs and sold Deutschmarks for spot value, and then bought the Deutschmarks back and sold francs for some forward date. The result was to push up the forward discount on francs (as well as to support the franc spot rate), which led to very high euro-currency interest rates at the very short end of the spectrum – as much as 10,000 per cent for overnight money, which implies an actual interest cost of some 30 per cent per day. This clearly made it prohibitively expensive to speculate against the French franc by going short of it, as this is exactly equivalent to having a loan in francs with a matching deposit of Deutschmarks.

In normal circumstances such action would be well nigh impossible because it would cripple the domestic industries if interest rates were pushed to these levels for even a very short space of time, and the average voter would not take kindly to seeing his borrowing costs take off in this way. However, exchange controls in France at that time were so tight that it was virtually impossible to transfer funds from the domestic market to the euro-French franc market. Consequently, nobody was able to borrow domestic francs and re-deposit them in the euro-French franc market (at least not legally and without the aid of a large suitcase!). Thus the two markets were isolated from each other and domestic French rates were very largely unaffected by the action of the authorities. Therefore, at that time the link between interest rate differentials – at least from a domestic market point of view – and forward exchange rate margins was broken.

A second exception is where the imposition of exchange controls is expected or anticipated. In these circumstances there may well be a flight of capital away from the country in question, though not necessarily away from the currency. If the money has already reached the euro-currency market, then it will generally be outside the scope of any regulations which very rarely are retrospective. Consequently, at the time of the flight, rates in the euro-currency may be considerably lower than those in the equivalent domestic currency market, reflecting the excess supply of funds and the relatively minimal demand for funds in the euro-currency market.

Yet a third exception is where there are controls placed on the domestic market. For example, these may take the form of liquidity requirements or credit controls. In normal circumstances this will do little more than widen the spreads in the domestic markets as compared to the spreads in the euro-markets (reflecting the cost to financial institutions of these restrictions), which are very largely devoid of such restrictions. However, if the controls on the domestic market become too onerous, there may be an exodus of funds to the euro-currency market, leading yet again to the development of a gap between domestic and euro-rates.

Although these three types of exception can occur, they do not occur regularly in the markets of the most heavily traded currencies. In the vast majority of cases and for most of the times, the relationship between interest differentials in both the domestic and euro-currency markets and the forward exchange rate margins does hold.

Are forward rates the markets' prediction of the future?

The forward rate is of course made up of two rates – the spot rate and the forward margin. Thus if the forward exchange rate is to be a prediction of the future, as seen by some weighted average of the market, then one or other – or possibly both of these rates in combination – must reflect the market's forecast.

1. The forward margin

As we have seen, arbitrage demands that the forward margin must more or less equal the interest rate differential between the two currencies. Thus it implies that for the forward margin to be the expectation of the future rate, the market must in some way be able to manipulate the interest differential.

There have been cases in the past where the above has pretty well unambiguously been true, but in such cases there have been special reasons why this has been possible. An example we have already touched on was French franc forward rates at the time of an anticipated devaluation within the EMS in March 1983. In this case the forward discount was pushed up in expectation of the devaluation, although as it turned out the discount was far more than the actual devaluation. However, the important point was that exchange controls effectively isolated the French domestic market from the euro-French franc market, and the French authorities were able to acquiesce to the market's movements (in fact they were able to encourage them) without doing much damage domestically. But in those economies where exchange controls are not effective – or do not exist – there is no such possibility of isolation.

In Chapter 5 on rational expectations, it was argued that this did not matter, but in certain circumstances it was possible that interest rate differentials would be determined by the forward rate. It is right to acknowledge the validity of this argument, but at the moment, and over the 16 years or so since the advent of floating exchange rates, it is apparent that the authorities of individual countries jealously guard their right to interest rate manipulation in support of other monetary control techniques. Therefore, for now, practical considerations dictate that interest rate differentials do determine forward margins and not the other way round.

2. The spot rate

The spot rate is the price which equates demand and supply for a currency at any point in time. However, we have already seen that one of the major factors in determining this equilibrium between supply and demand is the expectation of the market of where the rate is going. Clearly, then, in some sense the spot rate is the market's forecast of where the rate is going to be in the future – rational expectations demand this. The snag is that the market's time-scale of the future is very short term – if not instantaneous – and is ever-changing. The spot rate, then, is the market's prediction of the future, but that future only really extends to the next increment in time and is heavily dependent on all information known at the time, which as we have seen does not equate with all relevant information in most cases.

This is not to say, however, that there are not those in the market who take a view of a currency's movements for much longer periods, and who are prepared to stay with their position even if it temporarily goes wrong. While their view of the future is also reflected in the spot rate, the effect tends to be swamped by those speculators whose time-scale is much shorter. Individual long-term investors are important in the long term, but are less important in fixing day-to-day exchange rate movements.

3. The combination of spot and forward margins – the outright forward

If it is not the forward margin nor the spot rate that is the market's prediction of the long-term future, could it in fact be the combination of the two – the outright forward rate? Inherently there seems little to suggest that this should be the case because the reasons for either part moving seem so far removed from a long-term market prediction of the future rate.

But first, as we saw in Chapter 5, the rational expectations thesis does suggest that in a rational market – which the foreign exchange market is meant to be in terms of efficient use of information – some such relationship should exist between market expectations and forward rates. Statistical evidence has shown that the forward rate is a good predictor of the future rate in the sense that it is as likely to be too high a predictor as it is to be a low predictor. However, this does not mean that it is a good predictor of the future rate if we take as a measure of a good predictor, the minimum variation from the actual of the predicted rate. In fact this is fairly obvious if we consider how volatile spot rates are. As the spot rate moves, so must the outright forward rate, unless there is a compensating movement in the forward rate. As the latter is interest-rate related, it seems rather far-fetched to suppose that the forward margin would move in this compensating way. Therefore outright forward rates are likely to be as volatile as spot rates, and hence are unstable predictors of future trends.

Second, since the forward margin is calculated from interest rate differentials, the margin for a given period must reflect the difference in yield curves for the same period. In most cases the gap between two yield curves is likely to be fairly stable, and hence the forward margin will increase as a function of time. (Note: this is because forward margins strictly reflect the difference in interest rate costs rather than the interest rates *per se*, and thus the longer the periods of the forward margin, the greater the interest cost if the gap between the two interest rates remains the same.) As this is the case, then the forward margin will tend to move in the same fairly smooth trend as cover is calculated further forward (Table 10.1).

In the real world, exchange rates do not move in smooth long-term trend lines for periods that could extend over several years in those currency pairings which have liquid markets up to several years forward. Therefore on this basis, too, forward rates seem likely to be inaccurate predictors.

Overall it does seem that actual forward rates are unlikely to provide a guide to where the rates will be at some future time, although it should be stressed that they can still be used as a yard-stick for determining the success of exchange-rate hedging decisions, because they are known in advance and can actually be achieved, whereas future rates must obviously always be uncertain until they actually occur. Therefore the forward rate is a base-line from which to measure the improvement that hedging decisions have made. After all, if a

Table 10.1   The relationship between the forward exchange margin and interest differentials

Period	Forward margin United States dollar/pound sterling ($ premium)	Equivalent annualised interest rate (%) difference	Pound sterling interbank offer rate (%)	United States dollar, interbank offer rate (%)	Difference (%)
1 month	0.0055	3.626	13.00	9.375	3.625
2 months	0.0120	3.970	13.125	9.1875	3.9375
3 months	0.0175	3.863	13.1875	9.1875	4.00
4 months	0.0230	3.813	13.1875	9.1875	4.00
5 months	0.0280	3.717	13.1875	9.1875	4.00
6 months	0.0335	3.711	13.1875	9.1875	4.00
9 months	0.0477	3.533	13.0625	9.1875	3.875
12 months	0.0598	3.333	13.00	9.375	3.625

Note: Based on a spot US$/£ exchange rate of 1.8555 (rates taken 1 December 1988)

company chooses not to cover forward it does pay the price of reduced certainty in its base currency of future cash flows.

Conclusion

The forward margin market is largely a market based on interest rate differentials, a phenomenon that must be true if arbitrage is not to be continuously available. It is therefore unlikely to represent the market's expectation of future exchange rates. The only way in which this could be the case would be if forward exchange rates caused changes in one or other of the country's interest rates. For all practical purposes, in virtually all major countries, interest rates are directly and heavily influenced by governments. In these circumstances it seems unlikely that forward margins can dominate interest rates. It is much more likely that the relationship is the other way around.

In fact, if the forward rate does tell us anything, it is because its value is heavily dependent on the spot rate. Chapter 5 suggested that this should reflect market expectations, and nothing in this chapter has weakened the case for viewing the spot rate as being where the market expects the rate to go – albeit that there will be an allowance for interest differentials. An allowance seems a far cry from expectations.

11

IS THE FOREIGN EXCHANGE MARKET JUST A GAME?

Economic theory has concentrated on the fact that the foreign exchange market is perfect and, as we have seen, it also concentrates on the price (or the exchange rate) being the one at which supply and demand are in equilibrium. Modern approaches concentrate more on expectations and the price at which the stock of assets (currency) is willingly held. As we have also seen, supply and demand will only balance for the briefest possible moment. Economic theories have an important place in determining how supply and demand will change over medium- to long-term horizons and asset-market-type approaches explain why the path to equilibrium is not smooth, but both are of limited use when asked to predict how supply and demand for a particular pair of currencies will change in the next instant.

Given the short-term restrictions on the usefulness of economic theories, it may be useful to explore an alternative approach – that of game theory.

Game theory

Game theory attempts to model the way decision-making takes place in real situations. It examines how conflicts and cooperation may influence decisions, and how participants (players) can maximise their rewards, while at the same time minimising their risk of loss. Clearly, the two objectives are not possible at the same time – or at least are very rarely so – but game theory seeks to analyse the trade-offs that can occur between the two.

The idea of trading-off rewards and risks looks to be very much the sort of activity for players in financial markets, not least the foreign exchange market, so it is not surprising that game theory is one approach being used to model these financial markets. In a book of this type it is not intended that the subject be covered in depth, but rather that the ideas are introduced and some of the possible conclusions assessed to see if they can provide us with useful guides as to how supply and demand may alter in the very short term.

Zero-sum games

A zero-sum game is one in which for every winner there must be a loser, or, to put it another way, no matter how skilful the participants, no extra value can be added to the game. There are many examples of such games and economics abounds with them. In particular, financial markets would seem to fall into this category since, unlike many other forms of economic activity, they cannot add to 'world wealth' directly. They may of course do so indirectly by encouraging new developments, more efficient manufacturing, or more productive investment.

The foreign exchange market is certainly a zero-sum game. No matter how well the players devise strategies and tactics, the amount of value within the market will remain constant. After all, a profit made in one currency must mean a corresponding loss in the contra-currency for some other player. In the context of the foreign exchange markets, players would encompass all those who need to carry out exchange transactions, be they very large (as in the case of banks taking daily trading positions) or be they the very smallest personal transaction (e.g. a holidaymaker off on a package tour to Greece). Thus for all the players there can be no overall result other than zero.

This is not the same thing as saying that all players have an equal chance of winning. Far from it – the skill of the individual, his power in the market, and the accuracy of his information sources will all play a part in determining who wins and who loses. In addition like all good games there will also be the element of chance – for example being caught in the wrong position at the time of some completely unpredictable event such as the assassination of a major political figure.

The major problem with a market such as the foreign exchange market is that the number of players verges on the infinite, which makes the mathematics associated with the elements of game theory extremely complex and certainly puts them outside the scope of this book – and probably this writer! However, even a simple understanding of some of the rules may help us to understand just a little bit more about how the foreign exchange market works.

Rules of the game

The economic theories that we examined in the first part of this book are all based on one major assumption, i.e. that no one individual's actions can influence the outcome. In other words, the setting of an exchange rate is independent of the actions of any individual, and is based on an infinite number of decisions which are themselves based on rational decisions taken on examination of the changes in fundamentals and on all the information available. There is a good case for saying that for longer-term movements or trends, this is a very reasonable assumption, but it seems far less correct when applied to short-term movements in exchange rates.

From a practical point of view it seems less reasonable to assume that individual decisions cannot have a bearing on very short-term movements in the exchange rate. Unlike many other prices, exchange rates change more or less instantaneously, and again unlike many other prices – even in financial markets – it is difficult to determine some underlying value from which it would seem foolish to deviate too far.

If we then relax the assumption that no individual can influence the exchange rate, much of the earlier economic work loses some of its validity for explaining short-term changes in exchange rates. Game theory, which makes no assumption – indeed it is based on the probability that individual decisions can and do influence the eventual outcome – would seem to have an important part to play in our analysis.

If individuals believe that they can influence the outcome, then they will behave in quite rational ways, although these will not necessarily be rational from a fundamental viewpoint. Remember in Chapter 8 we said that the objective of dealers is to make profit and not to move exchange rates onto their long-term trend. In the context of game theory that makes perfect sense. If a dealer thinks that he can raise his chances of winning by making a particular decision, then he will be entirely rational in doing so. However, his decision will be based on a number of factors not necessarily related to the underlying fundamentals, or even to the information available.

1. The skill of the player

All good games have relatively simple rules, but at the same time are difficult to play because the availability of different strategies and outcomes make the possible outcomes of any game almost infinite. If, then, we reduce the part that luck plays in the game, the chances of a skilful player beating an unskilful one will be much increased.

The foreign exchange market does have simple rules – in the spot market they can be reduced to buying and selling different currencies at different rates. The outcomes could also be reduced to two or three – winning, losing or breaking even. However, the lack of alternative outcomes disguises the fact that the routes to these outcomes are many and varied. Luck must play a part in exchange rate movements – after all, nobody can predict totally unexpected and random events. But the role of luck is less significant than many think. In particular, the vulnerability of any player to the unexpected can be reduced and controlled, and the correct use of information can greatly enhance the chances of winning.

It could be argued that as there are so many players in the foreign exchange game, the impact of any individual player cannot be very significant. In fact, the number of truly important players at the very short end of the market probably numbers less than a hundred for each of the major currencies in any one time zone. Within this number there will be a hierarchy, with some dealers having a much higher reputation than others. If one of this group is seen to take a particular decision to buy or sell a particular currency, then the resulting impact on the market will be much greater than if one of the less significant players should take the same decision. Just like any other walk of life, there is always a great temptation to emulate the most successful. There will of course always be new dealers breaking into the ranks of the great, but in general (although one can always find individualists who are an exception to this rule), they will make more of an impact if initially they have built up a reputation by following the successful. However, the skill of the dealer is not the only important influence.

2. The power behind the dealer

There are many games – most notably those in which an element of gambling is involved – where those with the most to stake will increase their chances of winning in the long run. The corollary is of course that those who can afford to lose the most will have a distinct advantage over those who can afford to lose the least.

Similar considerations apply in the foreign exchange market. Those who can take the biggest positions in any currency will enhance their chances of getting the movement right. If foreign exchange traders held their position for too long, and it did not coincide with the changes in the underlying fundamentals, then, given the perfect nature of the market, they could not hope to win. However, dealers do not take long-term views. They are concerned only with the very short term, and in this context any large position that they might take could completely overwhelm the remaining supply and demand in the market. This is not to say that they will always win. They may choose the wrong moment when a number of smaller players have opposing views and will all be ranged against them in such a way that they are now overwhelmed, or it may be that a new piece of information becomes available unexpectedly. It is in the nature of things that such coincidence is not likely all the time (unless an element of collusion is in force), and unexpected information will, by definition, be as likely to be favourable as unfavourable, but this type of outcome does not invalidate our assertion.

There are other reasons why power and size are important. Resources other than speculative money also play a major part. If a dealer can call on the support of many colleagues, then he will be able to contact many other dealers more or less simultaneously, and consequently will be able to undertake far more deals before the market fully understands what is really going on, than will individuals who try to do the same thing, but on their own. Also, working for a larger organisation he is likely to have better information sources and, as we saw earlier, good and timely information is vital to the dealer.

But perhaps one of the most important aspects of power in this context is the power of exchange flows. By that I mean that a dealer who is seeing major movements (in whatever direction) across his book will be gaining priceless information about what is going on elsewhere in the market. Furthermore, increased turnover has a tendency to increase the chances of profit – the effects of bad decisions tend to be reduced. A dealer with large volumes of business is in a much better position to reduce his risks, which as we saw is one of his two objectives (together with making a profit).

3. Conflict or collaboration?

One of the main themes behind game theory is the idea that in the real world there is not the search for profit maximisation that traditional economic theory would have us believe. In particular, participants in any market tend to discover that there are certain strategies which will increase their chances of winning, but will not necessarily maximise their winnings. Game theory goes into some detail in working out pay-off matrices which are fairly simple to understand when the game only has two players, but are much more difficult to appreciate when the number of players is potentially infinite.

It will be sufficient for this chapter merely to introduce the ideas of minimax and maximin, and then try to relate them to the foreign exchange market. For these terms to have any meaning, the game needs to have a zero sum – in other words for every winner there must be a loser, or a combination of losers. In the foreign exchange markets such a condition exists because no global added value can be created directly from mere dealings in foreign currencies.

A maximin is simply that combination of pay-offs which will give a player the maximum value of minimum outcome, no matter what his opponent does. In other words, he can give himself the maximum chance of making a minimum acceptable profit. This is not the same thing as maximising the outcome. In a way it is reducing risk while seeking to make some profit. The minimax is the same decision as the maximin but for the other player. That is, it will be the strategy which minimises the chance of making the greatest profit.

It seems plausible that players in many games, not least foreign exchange, will find the maximin strategy a highly acceptable one. It is not so easy to see why they should adopt a strategy that cannot maximise profits. However, the two are really the same outcome seen from two different directions, and, as we shall see, there does seem to be more than a hint that foreign exchange dealers do indeed operate some form of maximin strategy.

In the case of the foreign exchange market with its many players, there is little point in trying to establish what any particular player's maximin or minimax might be, but this does not negate the idea that participants in this market will be adopting a strategy somewhat similar to this. Many (and probably most) participants in the foreign exchange market are not dealing on their own account, but, rather, for some larger organisation. Their performance and probably their rewards will be linked to the profits (however measured) that they generate for the organisation. However, on a day-to-day basis they will be looking to turn in regular profits, rather than for spectacular swings from profit to loss which might still generate greater profits at the end of the day. They will look to lower the pressure on themselves by reducing the risks of a loss, while still generating a satisfactory level of profits. There will of course always be high risk takers in any profession, but even in the foreign exchange market they will tend to be in a minority.

Given the above it seems highly likely that a dealer will be operating a strategy which does not seek to maximise profits, but will be looking instead to maximise the certainty of satisfactory profits. He is thus likely to be using some sort of minimax strategy. This will show itself in a number of ways:

1.   A dealer does not look to find peaks and troughs; he looks to take advantage of as much of a trend as possible, but he is realistic enough to realise that the odds against him of finding turning points are too high and too unpredictable to make that an attractive strategy.

2.   A dealer must know when to take both profits and losses. Alternatively, this could be rephrased as not holding on to any currency position for too long. A good dealer knows when to swallow his pride and admit that he was wrong.

3.   It is important to have the right ideas just before they dawn on everyone else. To have the right ideas too prematurely almost certainly means that losses will occur initially, and although the position may turn out to be correct and profitable in the long run, that is too great a time-scale for most dealers.

4.   Foreign exchange profits can be formulated in many different ways. In the case of a dealing room it will be simply whether or not the room has made money in its base currency during the day. In the case of a corporate attempting to hedge a particular exchange rate risk, the emphasis may be much more on reducing risk rather than looking to squeeze out a little more profit.

If we accept, then, that dealers do not look to maximise profits, the implications for exchange rate movements are enormous, and may go a long way to explaining some of the many inconsistencies that seem to occur. First, however, it is important to look at the different measures of profit that are being used, to see why even in a zero-sum game, there may be times when everyone really is a winner.

Foreign exchange profits

We have said before that the foreign exchange market is a zero-sum game, and that for every winner there must be a loser or a combination of losers. Therefore, it would seem to be a paradox to suggest that there are circumstances in which everyone – well, almost everyone sees themselves winning. The key is in the phrase 'sees themselves winning'. In other words, it is the player's perception that he has won, when a more objective observer might say that he had in fact lost. Is this no more than an individual confidence trick? Not really, it all comes down to the fact that different players have different views on what success is. A look at the objectives of two major groups of players will help to clarify the issue.

1. The speculators

A speculator's objective is to end the game period with more of his base currency than he started with; it is difficult to conceive of a simpler measurement of success. However, to the extent that the base currency is weakening against other currencies, it may be possible to achieve success in these terms, even though if the base currency were to be given a trade-weighted exchange rate, there might be less at the end of the day than at the beginning. With this one qualification the speculator measures success on a simple profit basis.

2. The hedgers

One of the major functions of a hedger is to reduce risk, although this is not to say that there is no concept of profit in what he does. However, he does not look at opportunity profits and losses, but at profits in relation to what is going on elsewhere in his business. For example, if a UK exporter sells goods to a company in the USA in dollars and the exchange rate on which he based his pricing is $1.50, then if he can cover his position at a rate below $1.50 – say $1.40 – he will view this as a gain, and his hedging as successful. If the rate falls further to, say, $1.30, he has clearly lost an opportunity of making an increased profit. In most cases, although he may be disappointed, he is unlikely to view his exchange rate deal as one that produced a loss. The opportunity lost is profit for somebody else and accounts for the fact that both sides of the same exchange rate deal view their decision as a profitable one. In addition, the hedger may view profit as beating his performance yardstick, i.e. the spot, or forward rate, or anything else that might have been chosen.

The above example does not invalidate the concept of the foreign exchange market as being a zero-sum game, but it does suggest that the motives of the different players in the game differ widely. The consequence for exchange rates is impossible to predict save to say that such factors do go some way to explaining some of the more illogical exchange rate movements when viewed from an economic fundamentals basis. To this extent it corroborates the views of the asset market approach. Where it differs is in the appreciation of the effect of individuals and not just the aggregate of individuals on the market.

Summary

The suggestion in this chapter that foreign exchange markets are a good example of an application of game theory does seem to have enough anecdotal evidence to at least give it a validity equating to some of the economic theories that purport to explain exchange rate changes. It would not, and should not, alter one of the major premises of this book, that economic fundamentals are very important when explaining long-term exchange rate trends. However, it does place a question mark over those who think that markets will constantly endeavour to move exchange rates towards some long-term equilibrium. There is nothing in game theory to suggest that this will happen, and while supply and demand will always be equated at the price, there is no suggestion that the changes in supply and demand in the short term will be towards the equilibrium.

The theory would, however, give some added explanation to what sometimes seem almost random exchange rate movements described by economists as 'shallow market thinking', or some other pejorative phrase. Such movements may not be predictable under economic theory (even when viewed as a reaction to a new piece of information), but they are nevertheless very real, as is the thinking behind them. It has always seemed strange that economists praise the efficacy of a perfect market on the one hand, but criticise the participants in that same market on the other hand for not appreciating the 'correct' movements required to put currencies back on the even keel that they deem appropriate.

12

NEW INSTRUMENTS AND THEIR EFFECTS ON THE FOREIGN EXCHANGE MARKET

Essentially, dealing in foreign exchange relies on a number of simple concepts, as does hedging of a foreign exchange exposure. Basically one can say that all decisions are based on the propositions: buy, sell, lend, borrow, now or in the future. The fact that the ideas are simple is not the same thing as saying that making the right decisions at the right time is at all easy – far from it. Nevertheless, the ideas are simple and until recently the available tools with which to carry out these decisions were in fact simple products – probably little more than the use of spot and forward foreign exchange markets, and the ability to borrow and deposit in different currencies.

With the advent of floating exchange rates, the removal of many countries' exchange-control regulations, and perhaps most important of all the internationalisation of the world's financial markets, there has been a move towards the production of more and more sophisticated instruments to make dealing and hedging much more complex, but hopefully more efficient, although sophistication can sometimes overshadow efficiency.

The purpose of this chapter is to see whether the advent of such instruments does indeed make decision-making or the markets more efficient, and to see what effects they might have on exchange rates in the short, medium and long terms. First, though, it will be useful to explain the main types of these new instruments, before going on to the effects on exchange rates.

Options

A foreign currency option gives the buyer of the option the right (but not the obligation) to undertake a certain exchange rate transaction at a fixed rate over some period of time. Thus the buyer of the option gains only rights but no obligations, while the seller of the option incurs only obligations and no rights. Not surprisingly, the seller of the option will expect to receive a fee for his trouble. An example may help to clarify this:

the buyer purchases an option which will enable him to sell dollars for sterling (the jargon is a 'sterling call') at a rate of $US 1.80, at any time in the next three months.

Outcome 1

The rate at some time during the option is $1.85.

At this point we can assume that, as long as the buyer is rational he will take up his option to sell dollars for sterling at $1.80 – thus showing a 'profit' of 5 cents. At the same time the seller of the option cannot walk away from his contract, and he will have made a 'loss' of 5 cents, his only compensation will have been the original fee he received when the option was bought from him.

Outcome 2

The exchange rate never rises above $1.80 during the period of the option.

In this case the buyer of the option will not exercise his option, but, rather, will let it lapse. If he had a real exposure to cover he could do so at a better rate in the normal foreign exchange market, or if he was speculating there is no chance of profit but his cost will have been limited to the original front-end fee. Here the seller of the option will have made no loss, and will have made a gain equivalent to the fee he received at the beginning.

At first glance it may seem that the buying and selling of options will have little effect on the foreign exchange market. To the extent that companies use options to hedge foreign exposure rather than more traditional techniques, there will be some effect on the leads and lags of how trade flows are hedged, but given the relatively small size of the options market (in the context of the entire foreign exchange market), the effect on actual exchange rate movements looks rather unimportant. However, we have made one explicit and one implicit assumption at this stage, neither of which are necessarily valid. The explicit assumption is that all buyers of options are hedging real exposures. The implicit assumption is that all sellers of options take no action to protect the risk they are running while the option is in force. Let us look at each of these assumptions in turn.

The buyers of options

Option buyers fall into two classes:

(a) those who are covering an underlying exposure; and
(b) those who are speculating on the expectation of a future currency movement.

Those who are looking for future currency gain may already have existed before the advent of currency options, but the arrival of the latter has enabled them to have a far more highly geared investment than was possible under, say, traditional forward contracts. At this point it should be mentioned that the majority of the options that are bought and sold can be exercised at any time during the life of the option (the so-called 'American option'), which will also mean that they will have a buy-back value (which can be zero if the exchange rate has moved in an unfavourable way). In addition, market traded options are negotiable and can therefore be transferred to anybody. Most speculators do not anticipate holding the option to maturity, but, rather, selling it back to the original seller, or to some third party. Thus there is unlikely to be a movement across the traditional exchange rate markets, which would be the case where the speculator had to deliver his currency if he wished to exercise the option and take his profit. The important point is that speculators who buy options will of course move the option price, but may not move the underlying exchange rate, especially if the seller of the option is doing nothing to hedge his risk in the traditional markets.

To the extent that the buyer of the option is covering an underlying exchange risk, it could be said that the option is replacing a transaction that would have gone through the traditional markets, and is therefore indirectly affecting the exchange rate. This assumes that the exposure would have been hedged if the option had not been available, and this is far from certain, particularly where the underlying exposure was contingent. For example, it might not hold where a company was tendering for an overseas contract, and where full cover was not possible without the aid of an option.

Buyers of options seem to have a relatively modest effect on the exchange rate, and to the extent that speculators move from taking positions in the traditional or cash markets, then there may appear to be a good chance for volatility in the cash markets to be reduced.

The sellers of options

The second assumption that we have made is that sellers of options take no action to protect their position. There are of course cases where sellers of options are in fact covering an underlying exposure, i.e. they sell an option against an exposure, knowing full well that they may lose the chance of extra profit if the option is exercised, but they are quite happy to accept that the fee they receive, together with the level they will have achieved for their underlying exposure, is quite acceptable. In this case – just as in that for option buyers who are covering an actual exposure – it can be argued that options are replacing access to the cash markets. Despite this their influence on exchange rates will be quite low. However, commercial sellers of options will be unlikely to work in this way. Despite popular belief, they are far from absolute risk takers. Indeed, they would love to be risk averse. This is clearly incompatible with selling options when there is no underlying exposure to hedge, so they will seek to reduce exposure. There will always be a cost incurred in reducing this risk, and it would be ludicrous to pay more for protection than you have received – so it is unlikely that a perfect solution will be achieved. There are three basic ways to reduce this risk.

The first is the normal actuarial approach of spreading one's business – in this case by writing options in several currencies, at different prices and on both sides of the deal (i.e. both buying and selling the currency). None of these will have any effect on exchange rates, although it may restrict the availability of options at certain times.

The second way to reduce the risk is to buy options from another seller (the equivalent of a book-maker laying off bets with another firm). It is reasonable to assume that the option market will be sufficiently competitive to prevent any one seller being able to charge a higher price for the same product. Thus it will be impossible to make any money on selling options if one's only method of reducing risk is by buying options, without taking a view on the way the exchange rate will move. Taking a view is not the route chosen by the risk averse.

The third way is by far the most important, and has by far the greatest impact on exchange rates. This is where the seller of the option actively hedges his option positions on the cash markets. Option hedging theory produces a formula which tells the seller of the option how much cover he should have at any particular exchange rate relative to the option price. For example, if he has sold an option to buy US dollars and sell sterling at $1.50, then – in very simple terms – the hedging ratios might look something like the following: when the actual rate is 1.46, 10 per cent, 1.47, 30 per cent, 1.48, 55 per cent, 1.49, 80 per cent, 1.50, 90 per cent, above 1.51, 100 per cent.

It is clear that the use of this technique will have an impact on the spot exchange rate in the cash markets, as option sellers cover or uncover their option hedges. The problem is that this very process of taking or getting rid of hedges may drive the exchange rate to the next trigger point where the next set of hedges will have to be activated. Obviously, this activity will not go on indefinitely, but it can certainly add quite a measure of volatility to a market which may already be experiencing considerable movement. If of course every option seller had a perfectly spread book, then there would not be such a problem. In the real world this is not the case, and the option books of all the option sellers tend to be bunched at the same levels, these levels being chosen for all sorts of reasons, but not least to coincide with the chart points that we will look at further in Chapter 13.

Summary of the effects of options

For some of the time, options may reduce volatility in the spot markets to the extent that it prevents a deal being struck when the option buyer would rather just insure his risk. However, in too regular a set of circumstances, the arrival of options has meant that sudden movements in exchange rates tend to be magnified as option-hedging strategies are operated. Such effects are unlikely to have any effect on the medium-term movement in the exchange rate, and therefore should not be taken into account when making economic forecasts, but they do need to be taken on board by anyone who is trying to find the best moment at which to make a particular deal.

Futures

A futures contract has many similarities with forward foreign exchange contracts in that it fixes a rate for the exchange of a given amount of one currency for another at a fixed date in the future. It therefore contrasts dramatically with an option contract, because with a futures contract there is a commitment to deal, whereas with an option contract, as we have seen, there is no such obligation. However, although it has many similar characteristics with forward contracts, there are some important differences which make the use of the futures contract quite different at times.

A forward contract is an agreement between two parties to undertake a particular exchange transaction. It is therefore very specific in every way, and is individually negotiated so that such variables as the amount, maturity date, exchange rate and even currency pairing are quite individual. However, a futures contract is an exchange-based instrument and is negotiable, so that its ownership can be passed on to any third party. It cannot be ignored, though, because as I have said earlier the buyer or seller of a future retains a liability to deal. Because the instrument is exchange traded, there must inevitably be a good deal of standardisation, and this will lead to contracts being written for a fixed amount, for delivery on only a few days in a year – normally one day a quarter, restricted to a limited number of currency pairings and to a few exchange rate levels – usually 5 cents apart. The attractions of the futures contract appeal to speculators for several reasons:

(a) the relatively modest amount of each contract;
(b) the negotiability of the contract means that delivery of the underlying exchange contract can be easily avoided by merely selling (although possibly at a negative profit) the futures contract before maturity;
(c) the high leverage obtained by the fact that only a small proportion of the underlying contract need be paid to the exchange as 'security';
(d) the fact that such contracts do not count as part of exposure to any bank, and therefore no bank limits are required.

The fact that futures are attractive to speculators does not in itself mean that they will have any effect on exchange rates. If they merely substitute for speculative positions that would have been taken in the cash markets, then there will be no effect. It is only where these instruments have increased business undertaken by speculators, or have encouraged genuine hedgers to take a more 'active' hedging stance that they can truly be said to have any effect.

On the second point, it seems unlikely that there has been much effect. Corporate institutions have not been major users of futures, although particularly in the USA, banks have used these markets rather more. However, even with banks it seems more likely that they have used the futures market as an alternative to the cash market. No, it is from the first point – whether more speculators have been encouraged to look at exchange rate movements – that most of the effect comes.

It would be far fetched to suggest that it is just the availability of futures that makes speculation more likely. Far more of a probability is the increasing volatility apparent in exchange rates over the past few years that has made exchange rates so attractive to those wishing to speculate. However, the existence of futures markets with their attractions has meant that speculators have found a very convenient vehicle.

Undoubtedly, the major futures market for currencies (if not for all futures) is in Chicago – the International Monetary Market (IMM). This market exists in a time-zone which is one hour later than New York. In itself this is not important, but the liquidity of the New York market does tend to dry up when the European markets close, so that for a good proportion of its day, the IMM operates in a relatively illiquid cash market environment. This enables speculators to assume more than their usual importance because there is no counter-balance from trade or longer-term investment decisions. Furthermore, futures markets (and not just those in currencies) have always been heavily dependent on the results of technical forecasting – which is hardly surprising given the importance of short-term movements to such markets. With technical analysis freely available (if not free!), most will be taking the same decisions at the same time, thus driving the rate somewhat further than it might otherwise go if the market was more liquid. As we have already seen in Chapter 8, the secret of being a successful short-term operator is to be right at the same time as – or only just a little before – the rest.

The above analysis may appear to be a criticism of the futures market. It is not. What it is trying to show is that when making dealing or other short-term decisions it is important to take into account movements that may or may not have already taken place due to decisions taken on the futures market. Because of the very short-term horizons of most operators in this market, it is extremely unlikely that the advent of futures markets will have much effect on longer-term movements in exchange rates.

Swaps

The concept of a foreign currency swap is very simple. It is to convert a currency to another currency at some point in time, with an agreement to reconvert back to the original currency at some further point in the future. The rates of both exchanges are agreed in advance. The product has been around for a long time, and is merely undertaking the two transactions at the same spot rate, with the further date transaction being adjusted for the forward margin. For example:

> Convert $US 1 million to sterling for spot value, and in one year's time convert the sterling back to dollars. (The exchange rate for the spot transaction is $1.80.)

The exchange rate for the transaction in one year's time will be at the same spot rate of $1.80, but adjusted by the forward margin to sell dollars in twelve months time – say at a premium of 4 ¢. The outright rate at which to sell is thus $1.76.

The main restriction to these types of transaction is that generally they will be bound by the length and depth of the forward market, which rarely extends beyond five years, and in many currencies does not extend even as far as one year. However, it seems highly probable that somewhere in the world there will be an equal (or almost equal) but opposite interest. Therefore, a market has grown up which tries to undertake this sort of matching. Forward margins, as we have seen, very largely equate to interest differentials and this 'matching' market has used this concept to present swap prices in a slightly different way.

Instead of adjusting the forward rate by the forward margin, both capital transactions are done at the spot rate. The difference in interest rates is settled on a previously agreed basis by means of a cash payment (usually annually) from one side of the swap transaction to the other. The main reason for this is that some of these pairings are for several years, and the payment of interest on an annual basis equates more fairly with normal practice elsewhere in the borrowing and lending market.

However, from the effect it will have on the exchange rate it matters little which type of swap is being used. The use of swaps enables companies to hedge long-term exposure problems in the sense that a currency which they do not need for the moment is nevertheless one they will require in the future. It seems likely, therefore, that it will reduce the reliance of these companies on the more traditional foreign exchange markets, where a sale now would be followed by a purchase later. It certainly enables companies to take a long-term view of their currency needs. It seems likely that the use of swaps – particularly long-term – will reduce volatility in the currency markets. Behind swap transactions will often be an investment or trade flow, so it would also seem likely that the use of swaps will, if anything, be efficient in moving currencies towards longer-term equilibria.

Other instruments

There are many other foreign exchange products around which masquerade under many different names, but in reality they are all derivatives of one or other of the foreign exchange products we have already looked at. This does not mean that they are not useful, but their effects on the foreign exchange market are likely to be roughly the same as those of their parent product. That is to say, to the extent that they encourage short-term speculation, they can be said to be likely to increase currency volatility. However, most of these products have been clearly aimed at performing a particular job, say hedging translation exposure, and are therefore more likely to be used by those who do have an underlying exposure to hedge. If this means that the product is used instead of traditional markets, there is likely to be little effect, but to the extent that they allow companies to take decisions that are more in line with their longer-term objectives, they could even reduce volatility.

Conclusion

That the growth of new products has had an effect on the foreign exchange markets, there can be little doubt. However, the major effects have been where the products have made life easier for the short-term speculator or, more usually, where the provider of the product has had to undertake more active hedging operations to hedge his newly created exposure. For many companies the advent of new products has enabled them to hedge risks that previously had to be either ignored or feared. Even with the almost exponential growth which we have seen over the last few years in these markets, their share in total foreign exchange transactions is small. It is the hedging of their positions by those who have sold these instruments that can destabilise currency markets in the short term.

Part IV

THE USES AND MISUSES OF FOREIGN EXCHANGE KNOWLEDGE

13

TECHNICAL ANALYSIS

Introduction

All the forecasting techniques that we have looked at so far have been based on economic theories of one sort or another. They have tended to work well when the forecast is covering the long term, and especially when we are trying to ascertain average exchange rates, but they do not perform well when it comes to forecasting the short term, or for making dealing decisions.

Technical or chart analysis concentrates only on forecasting the short term – in fact, very often, the shorter the better. It relies on no specific economic theories and instead suggests that it is wholly inappropriate to try to explain short-term movements in this way. There are too many interlocking factors at work to make such analysis a useful exercise. In essence, the technique relies on the belief that all known information is incorporated in the market view (an idea which is included in the asset market and rational expectations approaches) which produces the supply and demand conditions which themselves lead to the setting of the price or exchange rate. Examining the way these prices or exchange rates move over time provides the technician with the 'best' information there is for predicting where the rate is going over the short term.

The idea behind chart analysis is thus simplicity itself, but a whole industry has grown up and has introduced innumerable techniques where sophistication is often confused with complexity, and where sometimes the naming of a technique seems more important than its success in predicting what it set out to achieve. Nevertheless, from this complexity can be extracted a number of simple rules that can be usefully incorporated into forecasting methods for exchange rates. Indeed, since chart analysis is an integral part of the foreign exchange market it would be wrong to ignore it completely. If the methods do produce good results, then it is nonsense to decry them just because it is impossible to identify some underlying theory. Such theories provide comfort if they are available, but academic integrity comes a poor second to success in the eyes of foreign exchange traders – and rightly so. Broadly technical analysis can be divided into five areas, some of which need then to be sub-divided.

1. Trends

The idea that currencies do move along some sort of trend would seem to fit with economic forecasting techniques which predict currency adjustment over a period. (In Chapter 4 a time trend was incorporated into the monetary approach.) However, conflict arises when this trend is in the opposite direction to that expected using more fundamental or traditional economic-based research. This was of course the case in 1983 and 1984 when the US trade and current account deficits were pointing unequivocally to a fall in the dollar to a more competitive level, but the charts were pointing to further rises. The charts turned out to be the more accurate predictor for quite some time.

One of the first rules of chart analysis is 'the trend is your friend'. In other words, following a trend has proved a successful forecasting technique. This is especially true if the trend is relatively flat – that is to say it has a shallow gradient with respect to the horizontal. In these circumstances it is seen as sustainable whereas a steep trend line is regarded as volatile, and therefore as less sustainable. There are basically two simple ways of trying to discover such trends.

(a) Sloping lines on the price chart
If the exchange rate is plotted on a regular basis – say once a day or once an hour – then there are long periods when a trend will be observed. Chartists will seek to draw two parallel lines that encompass the currency movements, and will then predict that the exchange rate will continue to follow this 'channel' (see Fig. 13.1).

However, if we are in an upward-sloping trend formation and the exchange rate bursts out of the top of the range and looks to be forming a new channel, then this is seen by chartists as an early warning that the trend is about to be reversed. This is especially true if the exchange rate bursts out of the new channel formed in a further upward movement. Obviously, the same analysis, but in a reverse direction would apply if the exchange rate were in a downward-sloping trend formation.

(b) Moving averages
The principle behind this is that moving averages will smooth the day-to-day fluctuations out of the exchange rate, and will make it easier to identify the trend line. The choice of period for the moving average is a matter of discussion, but if the spot rate moves above the moving average line, then the currency is seen to be in for a further rise. Conversely, if the currency's spot rate falls below the moving average line, then the currency is set for a fall.

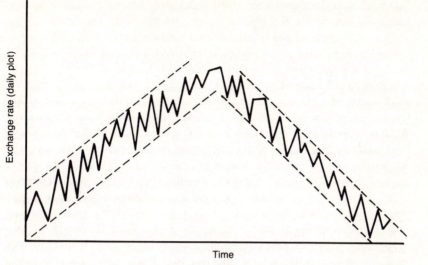

Fig. 13.1 Channels

Further sophistication can be added by introducing two moving average lines, one to determine the short-term trend – a relatively short-term moving average (say 5 days); and another to identify the long-term trend (say 20 days) – usually a much longer moving average. If the short-term trend moves above the long-term trend line, then this is seen as another positive signal for the currency, whereas a movement below the long-term trend line is seen as a negative signal. It is apparent that by using moving-average techniques the practitioner faces a dilemma. The more days he averages to obtain his short-term trend line, the more the day-to-day fluctuations will be averaged out. On the other hand, the longer the moving average, the longer it will take to pick up a change in trend direction and the more of the movement after the turning point will be missed. In any case, moving-average techniques ensure that the first part of any new movement is missed.

Thus if a new trend is set up the advantage will be to those using the shorter averages, but if the currency is moving in a choppy or whip-sawing market, then too short an average will mean that many false trends are identified and the speculator will wrongly go in and out of a currency incurring dealing costs and very likely a loss on each pair of deals. Nevertheless, the technique is very useful if a currency is in a prolonged trend and was very successful at the time of the dollar's rise in 1984 and 1985 for example.

2. Support and resistance levels

A second major chart technique is used to spot support levels – an exchange rate at which there seems to be regular demand for a currency – and resistance levels – a rate where the currency is persistently sold. The more times a currency is supported at a particular level, or the more times it fails to break through the resistance level, the more confident a chartist becomes that the currency will trade within the area bounded by these levels.

There may be sound economic reasons why a currency trades within a particular range. For example, currencies within the EMS must trade within bands, except when there is a realignment. Other examples of support and resistance levels are those where a central bank intervenes. A good example of this was sterling during most of 1987 and the early part of 1988, when the Bank of England regularly intervened to sell the pound to prevent it breaching the DM3.00 level, thereby establishing a very strong resistance at this level. over the same period sterling always received support at or just above DM2.95 and this established a support level. For almost a year the pound traded within these levels. As the significance of these levels are recognised, they can almost take on a life of their own. If investors are confident that a particular resistance level will hold, then it makes sense to sell the curency just before the resistance point is reached. Such selling does of course reinforce the resistance level. Similarly, it makes sense to buy a currency just above a support level.

If, however, a support or resistance level is breached, then a chartist expects the currency to move quickly to a level which is as far beyond the support or resistance level as the width of the previous band. If we take the example of sterling given above, once DM3.00 was breached, it was expected that the currency would soon reach DM3.05, the increase being the width of the previous band. One reason for this is that many investors will place 'stop-loss' orders just above (or below) the resistance (or support) level, so that if the currency does unexpectedly break through, their loss will be minimised. Thus when the currency does break through a resistance level, the market is swiftly confronted with a whole series of orders to buy the currency, which will drive it up even further. Reverse considerations obviously apply at a support level.

The longer a level has held as a resistance or support, the more likely that the subsequent move will be a large one. It is almost as if these levels have held back a pent-up demand, the most likely reason for this being that the longer a level has held, the greater the number of stop-loss orders in place, and hence the greater the push to the exchange rate from these orders. Again, the example of sterling given above shows that a resistance level that had held for almost a year, once breached, caused the currency to jump not to DM3.05 but, within two weeks, to DM3.10, and within six weeks to beyond DM3.15. Another point is that the more times a support or resistance level is tested and holds, the more important it becomes, and the more likely that any break through it will be a major one.

3. Pattern recognition

The idea behind this set of techniques is that in the history of exchange rates there are patterns which recur on a regular basis. If one is able both to identify significant patterns and to recognise them when they are repeated, it should be possible to predict the next major movement in currencies. The identification of patterns falls into two groups. The first group is based on the pattern indicating that a particular movement will be continued, and the second group uses patterns to indicate that a particular movement is at an end and is about to be reversed.

(a) Continuation patterns

Two simple ideas will give the flavour of how the methods work. The first is the 'flag' (see graph in Fig. 13.2). Here the idea is to identify a sharp movement – up or down – which will represent the 'pole'. This may then be followed by a parallel or downwards movement which is confined within two relatively narrow parallel lines – the 'flag'. A chartist would look for the exchange rate to break out of its flag in the same direction as the preceding 'pole' – in which case the next movement would be of the same height as the preceding 'pole'.

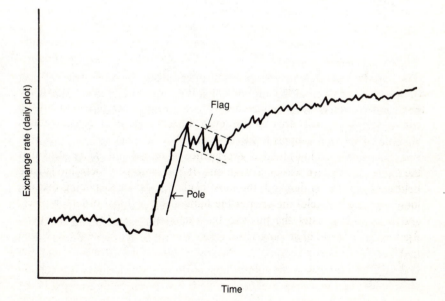

Fig. 13.2 Flags and poles

A second method is to spot triangles where the oscillation in the exchange rate decreases and is slowly confined to a triangle (see Fig. 13.3). Again, one looks for a break out of this continuous narrow range, in which case one would expect a further sharp movement whose size is determined by the size of the preceding triangle.

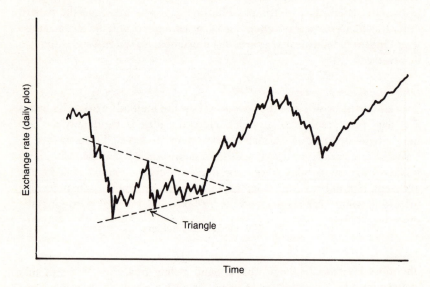

Fig. 13.3 Triangles

(b) Reversal patterns

The best-known of the reversal patterns and arguably the best-known, if least understood, of all chart techniques will suffice as an illustration. This is the head and shoulders formation to which Fig. 13.4 refers. At the end of a rising trend, a currency will have a set-back and will fall to establish the first shoulder. However, it will then rise again to a new 'high' to form the 'head'. It then falls back to a support level which is the same as that reached in the first shoulder – the so-called 'neck-line'. When this support level finally breaks, one looks for a fall equivalent in size to the height of the 'head'. Of course, in practice things are never as hard and fast as suggested here, with 'neck-lines' rarely flat and far more usually sloping, but nevertheless head and shoulders patterns are recognisable every now and again, and have proved to be a useful tool.

A head and shoulders can appear 'upside-down' when a currency is coming close to the end of a long decline, but otherwise it can be interpreted in the same way.

Pattern recognition is a valid area of study, but it is wise to beware of some of

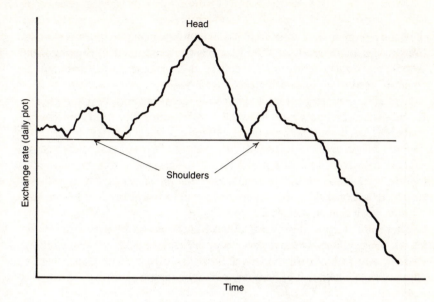

Fig. 13.4 Head and shoulders

the more mystical theologies that abound in this area. First, to be useful a pattern must be recognisable before the event that it is predicting takes place, and not after the event, when it merely confirms what has happened. Second, it must recur reasonably regularly to have any real relevance in forecasting exchange rates.

4. Momentum and velocity

Momentum is the speed at which exchange rates change value. The faster the rate of change, the more likely that a market is overstretching itself, and the greater the likelihood that a correction – often of quite a substantial nature – will occur. The secret is to know when the momentum has reached this level, and this largely depends on what has gone before. Velocity is based on the same idea but tries to average out some of the 'noise' that appears in pure momentum. When using velocity, the rate of change of moving averages, rather than the raw data is used.

Both methods can be used to establish overbought or oversold positions for a currency, but they are best used to confirm evidence from other techniques rather than as a forecasting tool in their own right. They are particularly useful for predicting in the short term – the period to which short-term speculative overbought or oversold positions are usually confined.

5. Cycles

The concept of an economic cycle has been fundamental to much economic thinking for many years, and the idea has been extended to commodities, equities and even interest rates. It would seem to make sense that similar ideas could be used when forecasting exchange rates.

Cycles, by their very nature, tend to be longer term, and consequently any period of fixed exchange rates will significantly reduce the period available for analysis. Thus the period from the end of the Second World War to the early 1970s is devoid of interest. Indeed, the evidence of cycles in exchange rates is somewhat sparse. Much play is often made of seasonal factors, be they end-month, end-quarter or end-year, but closer analysis shows that many of these so-called 'seasonal shifts' have more to do with hearsay than they do with any rigorous analytical or statistical approach.

There are 'very sophisticated' cyclical analyses, with perhaps the best-known being Elliot waves. However, they are really outside the scope of this chapter, and in any case there is a fierce controversy within the chartist industry as to whether they have any relevance, or are of any use.

Summary

Chart analysis and charting are often presented as being irrelevant because there is no underlying theory that one can point to. This is most unjust because the chartist will never have any great pretensions about the forces at work that change the supply and demand for a currency. Instead, he will emphasise that the best available information is summed in the present rate and how it has moved recently, though many still find this 'mumbo-jumbo' hard to swallow.

However, with many practitioners in the foreign exchange markets now actively using or perusing charts there is the possibility of self-fulfilling prophecy about some of the forecasts. To the currency dealer that is no sin as long as it allows him to make a profit. Charts are a source of information, and, like any other information in the foreign exchange markets, are valuable.

There is much to be said for keeping chartism simple. A stroll into some of the more esoteric areas means not only that there is more to assimilate and understand, and hence a risk of failing to see the wood for the trees, but also that fewer people are likely to be following the technique and hence it may be less powerful as a short-term predictive method. There is little doubt that support and resistance levels now play an important part in all currency dealers' thinking, and are used in particular when setting levels for stop-loss or stop-profit deals.

Like so much else in currency forecasting a selective approach which to some extent follows the dictates of fashion is often the most fruitful. But like any other fashion, it can be vital to realise early when the fashion has changed. For example, there has recently been a growth in 'real-time' charting systems. These use the same principles, but combine them in a proprietorial way. If you buy the package you get the results, which are instantaneously updated by real-time feeds to foreign exchange rates. The pictures are often better understood than any underlying reasoning, but as long as the particular model is fashionable it will be a reasonable short-term predictor because enough people will be following it. If it goes out of fashion, its predictive powers may well decline. It is therefore always much cheaper to discard a fashion too early than too late.

ECONOMIC FORECASTING OF EXCHANGE RATES

The first part of this book explained the various economic theories that are used in an effort to attempt to predict exchange rate changes accurately. From this it should already be clear that there is no one theory that as yet can be said to have solved the problem. Even if there was it would still be important to understand the limitations of the theory when it comes to predicting movements, rather than simply to explain what has happened previously. The purpose of this chapter is to explain what economic exchange rate forecasting is good at, and what it is not good at, and to draw from this the good uses and bad abuses of such techniques.

Economic fundamentals tell us about medium- to long-term equilibrium positions

Any of the theories predicting exchange rate movements will be predicated on the assumption that there will be a lag between cause and effect. There can be two reasons for this lag:

1. A delay in getting the economic data

It is self-evident that until the market knows that there has been a change in economic fundamentals it will be unable to start making the necessary adjustments to the exchange rate. If, for example, we assume that a market is basing its decisions on purchasing power parity, then it is not until comparative inflation figures are available that it can take the required dealing decisions. In other words, any expectations can only be based on known information, although the underlying change has already taken place.

2. A delay in economic changes feeding through to the underlying trade or investment flows

There is nothing in any of the economic theories of exchange rate determination that states a move to the long-term equilibrium position will be either instantaneous or straightforward. When a disequilibrium occurs this will feed through into the trade and investment flows eventually, but the effect will not be even, nor will it happen straightaway. An example will make this point clear.

If country A has an inflation rate twice that of country B, then its exports will become increasingly uncompetitive. However, this will not be a continuous process, but will happen in discrete steps. An exporter may decide to hold his prices for some time, taking the increased costs in his profit margin. The exports may themselves be far from price elastic, and consumer preference may mean increased prices will be willingly absorbed by the buyer. Finally, the effect will not be the same over the whole range of exports and imports.

From the above it is obvious that while the higher rate of inflation in country A must lead eventually to a deterioration in the trade position, the lags involved will be both long and variable.

It might be argued that investment flows will adjust more quickly than trade flows and therefore will be the mechanism that will adjust the exchange rate. This presupposes that longer-term investors are better judges than consumers of value as represented in a country's economy. It also presupposes that long-term investors will react to short-term economic changes. That seems unlikely: first, because short-term economic changes may not be a guide to the value of a long-term investment: and second, because the costs of unwinding investment decisions may be higher than the risks or costs of these adverse economic changes. By their very nature, investment decisions will have a long lead time, and it seems unlikely therefore that we can expect investment to take the lead in adjusting the exchange rate.

This leaves us with speculators or market operators to undertake the necessary adjustment. We have seen already that this group are out to make short-term profits which may bear no relation to long-term exchange rate movements. Consequently, while economic fundamentals will colour their judgement, speculators and market operators do not use them as the final arbiter in deciding whether to buy or sell a particular currency. In Chapter 11 I suggested that there was more than an element of game theory about the foreign exchange market. If this is the case, then there is no reason why short-term exchange rate movements will bear any relation to underlying economic fundamentals. This would only be the case if the risks of playing the game were heavily influenced by the long term. As we saw, they are not. Furthermore, the more modern economic theories emphasise the role of expectations based on all known information being correctly interpreted. Since the information contains neither all the relevant data, nor the correct interpretation of the data, these are assumptions that can not be made lightly.

Therefore if none of the three flows – trade, investment, and speculative – is certain to move exchange rates in the short term in line with the economic fundamentals, it must follow that economic forecasting must be of little immediate value in making short-term exchange rate decisions.

3. Which theory is correct anyway?

As we saw from the first section of this book, there are a number of different theories which claim to determine the exchange rate. It is by no means certain that they will all point unequivocally in the same direction. Indeed, past experience will suggest that they may in fact point in opposite directions, at least in the short term.

Over time all the theories have an element of truth in them, and it is not difficult to prove that over this long period of time the exchange rate will indeed move towards the level that the underlying theory will suggest. Thus, for example, a balance of payments deficit on current account will indeed lead to a weakening of the exchange rate, but the result is by no means immediate, as long as somebody is prepared to fund the current account deficit with capital inflows.

Leaving aside the well-known example of the USA in the mid-1980s, an even more startling example was Denmark through most of the 1960s and 1970s. During this period Denmark consistently ran a current account deficit, but the currency did not devalue to the extent that the theory would have suggested (see Table 14.1). Eventually, of course, the chickens did come home to roost, but the lag was many, many years more than one would have thought possible.

Table 14.1 The Danish phenomenon – current account deficits but relatively minor declines in the Danish krone exchange rate

	Current account United States dollar ($ m)	Danish krone/special drawing right (yearly average)
1970	−544	7.500
1971	−425	7.439
1972	−63	7.545
1973	−476	7.212
1974	−980	7.330
1975	−490	6.977
1976	−1914	6.979
1977	−1722	7.009
1978	−1502	6.904
1979	−2965	6.797
1980	−2466	7.335
1981	−1875	8.400
1982	−2259	9.199
1983	−1176	9.776
1984	−1637	10.615
1985	−2728	10.759

Thus with no one theory that has an unblemished track record when it comes to medium-term, let alone short-term forecasting, it is not surprising that few market operators pin their hopes on any one of them. What tends to happen is that theories come in and out of fashion, and it is important to be following the right theory at the right time. A fine example of this can be provided by the aforesaid US dollar during the 1980s. Even though the trade deficit was well into decline, the dollar kept on rising as investment flows continued apace into the USA. The theory in vogue was the genre containing asset and portfolio models. One was told of the safe haven currency status of the USA, the attractions of the strong government provided by President Reagan, whose support at that time was strongly behind a soaring dollar, and, finally, the benefits of nominal interest rates (which were very high) to the overseas investor; all of which determined that expectations were for the dollar to go on rising, at least for the immediate future.

Without any major shift in economic data, the dollar turned and began falling as fast as it had been rising. Suddenly, attention was focused on the dollar being overvalued on a purchasing power parity basis, and the whole market was talking of the impossibility of the USA being able to sustain trade deficits of this size indefinitely. Expectations were now unequivocally that the dollar had further to fall.

In retrospect it is easy to see the pressures building up on the dollar, and indeed at the time of the dollar's sharp rise, many economists were talking the dollar down. So were many dealers when it came to the longer term, and while few could see the dollar as high in twelve months' time, even fewer were prepared to be in the vanguard of dollar sellers. There is no virtue in being too far ahead of the pack, in the eyes of a foreign exchange dealer.

Thus we can see there is often a switch in the market's pet theories, and it is not surprising that in these circumstances, economic theories of exchange rate forecasting do not perform well in the short term.

Economic theories forecast average exchange rates

Not only do economic theories prove to be best when forecasting long-term exchange rate trends, they should be used to forecast average exchange rates over a period of, say, a month or quarter, rather than forecasting a spot rate at some particular time in the future. We have already seen in Chapters 8 and 9 that instantaneous movements in exchange rates are subject to a lot of 'noise'. This is because the exchange rate is the price at which supply and demand is cleared at a particular point in time. Not everyone, as we saw, will be supplying and demanding the currency with both eyes firmly fixed on the economic fundamentals. Most such decisions are firmly transaction based, either with a view to covering a particular currency flow, or because there is a short-term expectation that the currency is going to move in the 'right' direction.

It is obvious that it would be an extremely unusual event for these transaction-based decisions to happen in a continuous way. Thus at any point in time there may be a surplus of supply or demand which will temporarily boost or depress the exchange rate. This somewhat convoluted argument reiterates the point that short-term changes in the exchange rate may not always be towards the trend line. They can in fact take the rate further away from that line. However, if we average each of these exchange rates, the noise should average itself out, and we should be left with those movements that would be pushing the rate towards its trend line. The longer we make the average, then the more likely we are to remove the noise. Thus if, as we have seen, economic foreasting is trying to make predictions about the medium term, and particularly about trends, then it is more sensible to forecast by way of averages, rather than by estimating particular discrete moments in time.

How should economic forecasts be used when predicting exchange rates?

We have seen that economic techniques are best at predicting long-term movements in exchange rates, and are most reliably stated as averages rather than point forecasts. It is self-evident, therefore, that economic forecasting should be used where this type of forecast exchange rate is required.

1. Investment decisions

When a company is taking a strategic decision, say on investment in a new factory overseas, then it is quite clear that economic forecasting has a major role to play. In such decisions one is not really concerned with the day-to-day movements of an exchange rate, but with how the currencies perform over a period of some years. Consequently, it is important to attempt to discover the underlying trends, and to worry much less about what the exchange rate is on any particular day, although if the money is converted into the currency on one day, then that exchange rate will have a major once-and-for-all impact. However, if the spot rate moves adversely that day, it would not be appropriate to cancel the whole project indefinitely. This is the classic distinction between an investment and a dealing decision.

2. Balance sheet hedging

The whys and wherefores, and the pros and cons of balance sheet or translation exposure hedging are well outside the scope of this book. Suffice it to say that any company that has assets or liabilities overseas has an exposure to exchange rate movements between the currency in which the asset or liability is denominated and its base or reporting currency. It is of course entirely up to the company whether it should take any action to reduce such exposure, but whatever it decides to do, an important component underlying any decision will be a view on future exchange rate movements.

Most countries' accountancy conventions allow translation changes to be reported in one of two ways. Either the conversion rate can be that ruling on the day the balance sheet is drawn up, or it can be the average rate that has been in force throughout the period of the accounts. To try to forecast a point rate on a particular day is very difficult, although it should bear some relationship to the medium-term direction, but if one is using an average rate approach, then exchange rate forecasting using economic fundamental techniques is not only useful, but also very relevant.

3. Pricing decisions

Although economic theory seems to suggest that marginal cost pricing is the method used by almost all companies, practical studies that have taken place infer that many companies adopt some form of cost-plus pricing with, of course, one eye on their competitors, although the lag between loss of competitiveness and change of pricing policy can be both long and very variable.

For the vast majority of companies, exchange rates will be an important determinant of a company's prices. This can be directly if the company is selling abroad (no matter in which currency it is selling), or because part of the raw materials or components have to be imported (again no matter which currency they are in fact imported in). Alternatively, it can be indirectly, where a competitor's product is affected by exchange rate movements, which makes him either more or less competitive.

Because changes in prices tend to take place infrequently, not least because frequent price changes tend to be ill-received by the buyer, the effect of exchange rate changes on price can usually be more than adequately modelled by using medium-term trends or some concept of average exchange rates. In either case, economic forecasting is important.

4. Economic exposure decisions

Economic exchange rate exposure is not an easy concept to explain, but in very broad terms it can be said to be the susceptibility of a company's future cash flows to changes in exchange rates. There is no time limit to economic exposure, theoretically it exists through to infinity, but clearly the further into the future we go, the less meaningful become prognostications or forecasts of any variable. In addition, the further out we go, the more a company has control of its destiny in the sense that it can alter its production, perhaps from one country to another, it can withdraw from certain markets, it can change what it produces and sells, and finally it could decide it no longer wishes to exist, so that it can look for a purchaser or simply decide to go into liquidation.

Nevertheless, economic exposure exists for companies much further into the future than their normal planning process, and if one is trying to establish the vulnerability of a company to long-term exchange rate changes, then it is superfluous to say that a view of future exchange rates is essential. However, because the forecasts we are looking for are medium to long term, and would certainly be by way of averages, economic forecasting techniques are suitable once again.

5. Planning or budget decisions

Obviously this section encompasses much of the preceding four headings, but other decisions are involved, among which perhaps the most important from an exchange rate point of view is the setting of a planned or budget exchange rate for some future period. It can be argued, and indeed I would agree with the argument, that the setting of such a rate is irrelevant to the company's external performance. It is merely an aid to internal accounting.

However, in the real world, budget rates take on almost a religious nature, with operating companies believing that their performance measurement will depend on how they achieve their targets using this planned rate. Artificial the rate may be, but if people believe it to be more than that, and their decisions are influenced by what this 'internal' rate is, then it is important that some thought should be given to choosing a realistic or relevant rate.

Some view of future exchange rates must again be crucial, but because we are talking about average rates over a medium-term period, and are not trying to pin-point rates on a particular day, economic techniques are relevant.

Some companies do of course set planned rates which are in effect spot forecasts for a particular day. In these circumstances economic forecasting techniques are much less relevant, but then so too is the planned rate. It is probably more important to switch what the planned rate is intended to achieve more towards an average rate, rather than try to find some better forecasting technique.

What economic exchange rate forecasting is not good at

As we have seen, economic methods are least useful when trying to predict short-term movements, or when trying to forecast some exchange rate at a particular time on a particular date. There are thus two groups of decisions where economic forecasting should only be used when accompanied by a 'health' warning – and a strong one at that!

ECONOMIC FORECASTING OF EXCHANGE RATES   121

1. Dealing decisions

Because short-term market movements are influenced by many non-long-term factors, there will always be a great deal of volatility in such movements. Longer-term forecasting techniques cannot be expected to be helpful in spotting what are sometimes random movements because they are based on random changes in information. However, when one is dealing, it is important to have some understanding of what these movements might be, or at the very least a knowledge of what the worst case might be. Do not look at true economic theory for help, but look towards an understanding of what is determining market movements and market sentiment at that time. In particular, it is vital to understand what information the markets find crucial in establishing their expectations.

One must be especially careful of using short-term economic information, say the release of a particular monthly economic statistic, as an input into some established economic forecasting model. Just like any other information, it is the trend in such information that is important, not one-off figures.

Equally it is important not to ignore economic releases, but their effect on the market is more often of a short-term nature, and is more important for its effect on market psychology and expectations than it is as proof of some economic theory. Economic releases should be viewed as new information, but not conclusive information.

An example to illustrate the difference between dealing decisions and accurate economic forecasting may help at this point. The economic team may produce a forecast for the exchange rate between dollars and sterling for three months' time, but they should point out that they are proposing an average rate. Such forecasts are useful to know for deciding whether or not to cover the exposure forward, or leave any dealing decision to the date at which the exposure, say an import invoice, has to be covered.

Two points arise. First, it is quite conceivable that the forecast for the average exchange rate turns out to be absolutely accurate, yet on the day when the company would have covered the invoice on a spot basis, the rate turns out to be better than the forward rate that has been achieved. Because of high volatility, average rates cannot reflect individual points in time. Second, having decided to cover forward, there is still a need to make a decision as to the best moment to actually deal the forward rate. Again, the accurate three-month forecast cannot establish what is the best moment to deal. Only hindsight is able to achieve that, and hindsight is a singularly useless forecasting tool.

2. Point forecasts

If one asks an economic forecaster for his exchange rate forecast for, say, 31

December of next year, he should respond by giving a range. The cynic would say that he is merely raising his chance of getting the decision right. There may be an element of truth in this, but he should also be recognising that as he is forecasting an average, there is no way that he can or should suggest that he can accurately predict an exchange rate at a particular point. Even with a wide range, the actual rate may be outside, and yet the average forecast could still be correct. What he should do is establish the most likely risks to his forecast. Perhaps most fundamental of all, he should explain the assumptions behind the forecast. One explicit assumption is worth a dozen implicit ones.

Conclusion

This has been a long chapter, but it reflects the importance of the topic. Economic forecasting has received a lot of criticism because of its inaccuracy in forecasting exchange rates. Some of this criticism has been well directed, but some has more to do with the fact that both providers and users of such forecasts have misunderstood the value of the output.

Economic forecasting is not worthless, but it does lose value quickly if it is used for purposes for which it was not intended. Understanding what has happened in the past can help a company plan for the future, and in Chapters 1–5, explanations for what has happened were put forward. What the past tells us in particular is that exchange rate movements can be unexpected, unpredictable and highly dangerous. A healthy respect for exchange rates, and an understanding of the benefits of hedging uncertainty may be the two most important contributions that an economic understanding of exchange rates can bring.

APPENDIX

Economic indicators and their interpretation

Economic indicators are eagerly awaited by the market as being new information which may show signs of a continuing trend or, more significantly, may be the first pointers towards a change in direction. As we saw earlier, it is often not the actual outcome which interests the market but, rather, how it deviates from market expectations of that economic release.

There are many different economic indicators, not all of which are of interest at any one time. Much will depend on what the market thinks policy makers (e.g. government or monetary authorities) are looking at, and also which particular theory is the market's fashion at that time. This may lead to a figure from an economic release being interpreted in an entirely different way on different occasions.

For simplicity's sake the indicators have been grouped here into five sections:

(a) Inflation statistics;
(b) growth statistics;
(c) balance of payments statistics;
(d) money supply statistics and interest rates;
(e) leading indicators.

Obviously, different definitions are used by different countries, and I must admit to a heavy bias towards US and UK statistics. However, US statistics are by far and away the most important for the market as a whole.

Inflation statistics

The logical reaction to a bad inflation figure would be to sell the currency of the country with the high inflation rate. After all, purchasing power parity theory suggests that it is a fall in the exchange rate which will compensate for the increasing uncompetitiveness of the high-inflation country's goods. In some circumstances this will indeed be the reaction, but it is far from being the only response.

If the policy makers in the high-inflation country are motivated to take a very firm stand against inflation, the market may well respond to the anticipated policy action to the high inflation figure rather than the figure itself. Thus if the authorities are of a monetarist persuasion, then the expected response to bad inflation figures will be a rise in domestic interest rates. As we have seen from preceding chapters, relative interest rates are a major determinant of capital flows, and hence of exchange rates. Thus a high inflation figure which is expected to lead to a rise in interest rates frequently leads to a strengthening of the currency.

One cannot be hard and fast about which way the market will move in a given set of circumstances, or whether it will take the option of ignoring the inflation figure completely, either as being irrelevant or as already being built into the market's expectations. It is the feel of the market at the time which gives the best clues, particularly comments from well-respected economic gurus, or those who are in fashion at that time.

There are a number of different statistics used to measure inflation, and such a variety in itself produces another problem – which is the right one to use? There is no definitive answer, but the paragraphs below give a brief explanation of each, and what they are particularly useful at highlighting.

1. Gross national product deflator

This is the widest of all the inflation indicators. Very simply it is the figure used to deflate the rise in nominal gross national product (GNP) to produce the rise in real GNP. It therefore includes all aspects of the economy, but it is really an implicit measure of price rises, rather than a direct measure of price rises.

One major problem with the gross national product deflator is the delay in publishing the statistic, due to the complexities involved in measurement. It thus tends to be released rather later than other price indicators. A second problem is that the gross national product deflator is subject to many revisions, sometimes very extensive, not only in the few months after its first announcement, but for several years in some cases. Also, the figures are only issued quarterly, and thus are not sufficiently regular to become a real market plaything. However, in the USA where the figures are provisionally announced and then revised on a monthly basis, the quarterly series takes on some of the aspects of a monthly release.

2. Gross domestic product deflator

This is the version reported in the UK, and it excludes the effect of certain overseas transactions. However, because it is released each quarter and well after the event, it has never really captured the market's imagination.

3. Consumer price inflation (CPI)

This, as the name suggests, is meant to be the most clear representation of how inflation affects the 'ordinary man in the street' and attempts to measure the value of goods and services consumed in a country. It is constructed by regular surveillance of price changes of a weighted basket of goods. That is to say, the importance of each good or service to the average consumer is given by a weighting (regularly updated), so that goods which form a greater part of the household budget will have a larger effect on the index.

There are of course disadvantages to this approach. Perhaps the most important is that different sections of the community have very different spending patterns. Poorer members of the community are less likely to spend money on luxuries than a person in his peak earning period. A second disadvantage is that indirect tax increases raise the CPI, whereas direct tax increases do not. Yet it can be argued that the fiscal effect is the same, so why should one be interpreted as increasing inflation while the other is not?

Nevertheless, despite these shortcomings the index is widely referred to. One of the most important reasons for this is that the CPI is produced montnly, and with little delay. It is also subject to very little revision.

4. Retail price inflation (RPI)

This is more commonly used in the UK than the CPI. The controversial difference is that it includes the effect of mortgage interest rate changes.

5. Wholesale price inflation or producer price inflation

Wholesale (WPI) or producer price (PPI) inflation is another statistic that is collected on a sample basis and produced monthly. It measures the price of goods produced in the country. It is not affected by changes in indirect taxes, unless they impinge on the manufacturer and not just on the consumer. The PPI or WPI can be sub-divided in a number of ways. Figures published on the USA are examined in some detail by the market with price trends in individual sectors being well scrutinised. Various stages of production and commodity prices are very carefully analysed. In the UK the split tends to be between input prices – the cost of raw materials and fuel for manufacturers – and output prices – the cost of goods as they leave the factories. Whatever method is used it is clear that certain prices are more likely to be lead indicators than others. Thus in the USA raw-material prices, and in the UK input prices, are watched to provide early indications of changes in the trend of inflation.

However, an early indication is not necessarily the most accurate. For example, manufacturers may decide to absorb input price increases, either because of an increase in productivity, or to make their goods more competitive, or a combination of both. All in all PPI statistics tend to be watched closely by the foreign exchange market.

6. Earnings

Obviously, a key component of inflation is wage and salary increases. This statistic is particularly important in Europe (especially in the UK) where labour mobility is quite low, and where earnings increases have in the past often led to further price and wage increases as sector after sector of the working population has tried to 'catch up'.

One of the problems of looking at earnings figures is that they may not be really telling you what a cursory glance suggests. Some indices will include overtime payments and bonuses which may reflect a booming economy and/ or substantial increases in productivity. It is not the increase in earnings *per se* that is inflationary, but that part which cannot be justified by higher output, i.e. unit labour costs growth.

In the UK the average earnings series is smoothed to give an underlying trend. This illustrates another problem. In many economies pay increases tend to be bunched, and only a seasonally adjusted series can hope to eliminate this. But even seasonal adjustment will fail where there is a significant timing change in wage settlements and some attempt is made to capture that.

Clearly what really matters as a lead indicator is increases in wages per hour adjusted for productivity increases. This figure is unit wage costs, and in the UK it is released at the same time as the other earnings indices; and it is frequently ignored by the foreign exchange market!

Growth statistics

Economic growth is generally viewed as positive for an economy, especially if the rate of increase is faster than that of its competitors. From an exchange rate point of view, it should lead to inflows of capital to take advantage of the increased opportunities for investment return that faster economic growth should assure. Two 'health' warnings should be added to this assumption.

First, increased growth may lead to increased inflation, especially if bottlenecks begin to occur in production. This may force up the price of labour in particular, which will then lead to greater spending power and a rise in unit labour costs. Thus inflation can be caused by the cost-push effects of higher factor costs, and by the demand-pull effects of increased demand for a limited supply of goods.

Second, the increased demand for a limited supply of home-produced goods may also lead to a deficit in the current account of the balance of payments, as imported goods supplement home-produced products. This may not necessarily be a bad thing. If increased growth is attracting foreign private capital, then a deficit on the current account is inevitable if the government does not intervene on the foreign exchanges by selling the domestic currency. In addition, if the inflow of goods is mainly made up of capital goods, such as tools, then this can be interpreted as one way for the home industry to gear itself up to remove capacity constraints and to provide the goods that the increased home demand is clamouring for.

It was precisely this argument that was raging in the UK in the summer of 1988, when a very large deficit on the current account was seen as an inevitable adjunct to a booming economy, and was at least partly caused by industry investing in new capital goods. Critics of the government, however, suggested that an overheated economy was sucking in consumer imports, and that the situation was fast becoming out of control. This last phenomenon was at least partly acknowledged by the government who tightened monetary policy by pushing up interest rates, thus reducing the ability of consumers to borrow and hence spend.

What does all this mean for the exchange rate? In the first instance, strong economic growth on a relative basis should strengthen the exchange rate as capital inflows boost the currency. This should continue unless either the current account deficit cancels out the positive effect of the capital surplus, or if inflationary worries overwhelm the positive effects of a strong growth rate, and capital inflows either cease or are reversed.

However, in recent years the concentration on monetarist policies has added another twist, especially as markets have increasingly focused on the nominal returns provided by high interest rates. If economic growth is such as to suggest an overheating of the economy, and it is felt that inflation is about to pick up, and the current account to go into deficit, the currency will not necessarily weaken if it is assumed that the response of the government to these problems will be to raise interest rates. In these circumstances an overheating of the economy may well lead to the currency strengthening as interest rates either rise or are expected to rise. Thus like most economic indicators there is no one way that the market may look at growth statistics. However, it is still important to understand which of the indicators are the best in terms of indicating growth, and in terms of their effect on the foreign exchange market.

1. Gross national product (GNP)

This is the most comprehensive measure of growth in any economy. It covers all aspects of economic activity, and although in many sectors early measurements are made on an incomplete basis, it is hoped that the sampling method chosen is representative. Nevertheless, this does mean that the series is subject to revisions, which can be quite substantial at times. This is especially true in the USA where the statistics are produced earlier and on a more incomplete basis than those of many other economies.

The GNP figures are produced in both nominal and real terms. The ratio between the two is the GNP deflator (see above). For most purposes the importance of real GNP far overshadows that of nominal GNP. This is because growth in nominal GNP, which is merely represented by price increases, is the exact opposite of good for the economy or the currency.

From a foreign exchange market point of view, the GNP figures are very important and their effect is very great indeed. The fact that they are subject to revision makes their impact more volatile, although this is generally only of great importance if growth is close to zero, when the psychological impact of negative to positive growth or back again rather overwhelms the more long-term economic significance of the statistics. The major problem for the foreign exchange market is that the figures are only published on a quarterly basis. Hence the search for some interim indicators which provide a more regular and timely, if incomplete, picture of where the economy is heading (and where it has been).

2. Gross domestic product (GDP)

This is the UK version of growth statistics. It is very much the same as GNP, but there is a small deduction for property income from abroad. To all intents and purposes, however, it can be viewed as a direct substitute for or comparison with GNP in the UK and the USA, but in Ireland, for example, the difference can be as much as 2 per cent.

The UK experiences problems stemming from the fact that GDP is calculated in three ways: i.e. it is based on output, income and expenditure. This can lead to differences. In 1987, for example, the output measure grew in real terms by 4.7 per cent, while the expenditure measure grew by only 3.6 per cent.

3. Industrial production

This is probably the most important of all the coincidental growth series, and is an indicator of industrial activity. It is based on sampling techniques, and thus does not cover all areas of the economy. For example, in the USA it misses service and construction industries, among others. Also it has to weight the importance of various sectors and, by necessity, these weights must be based on the past. This is not normally so important because reweightings can take place on a regular basis, but at times the difference can be considerable. For example, in the UK in the late 1970s the importance of the oil industry was grossly understated because it was impossible to reweight the index sufficiently quickly to take account of the enormous expansion. Therefore, it is likely that new industries will be underrepresented in the sample, and declining industries will be overrepresented.

The corollary to this is that the constituent parts of the index are often more important than the whole. This is especially true in the USA where a comprehensive breakdown is available simultaneously with the overall press release, and where the minutiae of the different sectors are subject to close scrutiny by analysts. In the UK the rise and fall of the oil industry has been carefully watched.

As the statistics are released monthly they must be seasonally adjusted to be useful. Again, the seasonal adjustment must be based on the past, and therefore any change in seasonal pattern will not be picked up in the series immediately. Nevertheless, in general the seasonal adjustment techniques are both sophisticated and reliable.

Because of all the above, and the late arrival of more complete information, the series is subject to some revision, but is generally stable. Thus the foreign exchange market attaches a good deal of importance to industrial production. Its early release, and the fact that it is available monthly make it particularly important and eagerly awaited.

4. Retail sales

This, as the name suggests, is a series that measures final sales in retail establishments. It thus excludes sales by wholesalers to retail stores. Retail sales is another monthly series, but it is less useful than industrial production because it is far more unstable and is subject to very large revisions indeed. In addition, in the USA it is the value series that the market examines, not the volume series, and thus the picture is distorted by price effects. Also the seasonal pattern is unreliable.

Nevertheless retail sales is a regular measure of consumers' spending patterns, and despite its limitations it does have some utility. It becomes more useful when some of the more destabilising factors, such as automobile sales, which can be subject to violent swings because of promotions and discounting, are removed.

5. Automotive sales

This US data is produced in two different ways. The three major automobile companies publish ten-day figures three times each month. These provide the first indication of how this important component of retail sales is progressing. The second format is a monthly series which takes into account both domestic and foreign car sales to the USA. Therefore, at a time of changing import penetration of the domestic market, changes in the preliminary domestic data may over- or understate the monthly series changes. However, as we saw

above, automobile sales can be heavily influenced by special factors such as
sales promotions and/or discounting at variable times of the year, and the
series needs to be treated with caution by those who do not have a full
understanding of these special factors.

6. Employment and unemployment

Another monthly series that is an indicator of the robustness of the economy.
However, it may be even more important than this since unemployment can be
a very sensitive topic (and not just for those who are out of work), so that at
times this series takes on a political as well as an economic dimension.

In the USA the unemployment rate is based on a household survey which
measures the number of people in work, and those who do not have a job.
Some parts of the employment scene, notably agriculture, are highly unstable,
and although the data is seasonally adjusted, many analysts prefer to look at
the non-farm employment statistics rather than the total aggregate.

In the UK the series measures the number of people out of work by using
registrations of unemployment rather than surveys. There is also a series
representing notified vacancies left unfilled, but this figure probably
understates the unsatisfied demand for workers. The most unstable part of the
working population in the UK is school-leavers, and the series that excludes
these is the one most usually selected.

Too low a level of unemployed can be seen as evidence of capacity
constraints building up, but generally falling unemployment suggests a
speeding up in economic growth. Growing unemployment on the other hand
is clear evidence of an economic slowdown, and is generally bad for a
currency.

7. Durable goods orders

This is an American series which is produced monthly. Because it measures
orders and not deliveries, it is a leading indicator of economic growth. Durable
goods are defined as those with a life expectancy of at least three years,
and includes primary as well as finished products. The data shows the net
position between new orders and cancellation of those previously advised.
The total series can be heavily distorted by defence orders, which are neither
seasonal nor predictable. Consequently, the better indicator is seen as durable
goods orders less defence orders, announced as non-defence durable goods
orders.

The foreign exchange market does attach a good deal of weight to this
series, mainly because it is an early indication of economic growth. It is
nevertheless revised each month, and the market examines the net effect of
the revision and the new figure before making its judgement.

8. Housing starts and permits

Housing starts and permits are monthly American series which are seen as leading indicators of economic growth.

Housing starts is the number of new units – be they single or multifamily – started in a given period, but it only refers to private housing. 'Start' is defined as the beginning of excavation.

Housing starts may be heavily influenced by adverse weather conditions. Thus analysts factor bad weather into their expectations, and the series is difficult to interpret unless it is against this expectational background.

Housing permits refers to the number of permits issued by local authorities for new private housing projects. This obviously precedes housing starts, but there is an indeterminate delay between the granting of a permit and the actual building being started. Nevertheless, housing permits are an even earlier indicator of economic activity, but the figure may be artificially high, especially before an economic downturn, because not all permits will be translated into actual housing starts – a trend which will be exacerbated by an economy that is in decline.

9. Sales and inventories of single-family homes

This series is a follow-on from those above. It is a monthly report on new single-family home sales in the USA. It also provides data on the stock of new housing that remains unsold at the end of the period. In many senses this is a much more relevant series than housing starts and permits because it deals with both the demand for and supply of new housing, and gives a much better indication of the state of the US housing market. However, it is not a leading indicator, and to some extent is only a proxy for other coincidental data such as retail sales, which are seen as more important because of their scope. Thus the series does not generally grasp the attention of the foreign exchange market, unless something unexpected or sensational occurs.

10. Capacity utilisation

This is another monthly series which is expressed as a ratio between actual output and potential output. The ratio is expressed as a percentage. Potential output is the maximum output that can be generated with all existing plant and equipment working at a normal rate.

The series is an important one because it gives an indication of a potential overheating of the economy. Clearly, the ratio should never approach 100 per cent because it is highly unlikely that all production will be under equal pressure. Indeed, any figures near 85 per cent suggest that bottlenecks are building up. This is not necessarily a bad thing for the currency, as long as it is expected that action will be taken to raise interest rates to take some of the heat out of the economy.

11. United States factory orders and machine tool orders

These are two more orders series which can be said to be lead indicators of growth. The first measures both durable and non-durable goods orders, and is published some two weeks after the durable goods orders report, which it updates. The fact that it is an update or revision means that it gets much less attention from the foreign exchange market. The machine orders figures are a monthly report of a survey which is self-explanatory; in general, too esoteric a series to have much impact on the foreign exchange market.

12. Plant and equipment expenditures

This is a quarterly series which covers the expected new plant and equipment expenditures of all non-public sectors of the US economy. The fact that it is only a quarterly series and merely updates the earlier expectations (even though it may be a more accurate and relevant series) means that it tends to have little more than passing interest for the foreign exchange market.

13. Personal income

Personal income is one of two series that examine the money coming in, rather than the way in which it is spent. The series is monthly in the USA and examines all forms of income in the personal sector, the most important of which is earnings. Although the series is coincidental in terms of timing, it is eagerly awaited by the foreign exchange market as a measure of how well economic growth is proceeding. The series is quite reliable and only subject to minor revisions – very much another plus point.

14. Corporate profits

Corporate profits is a quarterly series which is published both in nominal and real terms and which measures the difference between revenues and costs. It is a very direct indicator of how attractive equity investment is likely to be to the investor, and thus it may give some clue as to the level of capital inflows or outflows.

Balance of payments statistics

Given that a whole chapter in this book was devoted to the balance of payments approach to exchange rate determination, it will be obvious that balance of payments statistics are always eagerly awaited by the foreign exchange market. After all, at the end of the day the exchange rate is determined by the supply of and demand for a currency which itself is determined by the flows identified in the balance of payments accounts.

Again as we saw in Chapter 2, it is by no means clear exactly which part of the balance of payments accounts is the most appropriate. It may well be worthwhile setting out the structure of the balance of payments accounts:

VISIBLE TRADE
INVISIBLE TRADE
        CURRENT ACCOUNT BALANCE
CAPITAL INFLOWS
CAPITAL OUTFLOWS
        CAPITAL ACCOUNT BALANCE
        ERRORS AND OMISSIONS
        BALANCE FOR OFFICIAL FINANCING

1. Visible trade (trade balance)

Visible trade is, as the name suggests, the trade in goods. As such it is made up of two distinct parts: exports and imports. Therefore the balance on visible trade is a difference. This rather self-evident point has an important follow-on; i.e. even quite small errors (in percentage terms) in the value of either exports or imports will have a much greater effect on the difference between them. It is thus not surprising that the series from any country can be quite distorted in this way. This distortion is not helped by the fact that both imports and exports tend to be very seasonal in most economies. Most sets of visible trade figures are seasonally adjusted. Nevertheless, this is an extremely difficult adjustment to make. To this must be added one-off distortions, such as exports or imports of major capital goods. In the USA this can often involve the export of, say, a number of large air-liners.

Despite all of these problems, the balance of trade is one of the most eagerly awaited figures in the foreign exchange market, apprehension being somewhat ameliorated by the facts that it is released monthly and that it is easy to compare the figures between one country and the next, and thus obtain some comparative idea of how trade is developing. (It is important to understand that the figures are rarely exactly comparable because of the differences in reporting periods between countries.) The foreign exchange market tends to react quite violently to a trade figure that is wildly different to that which has been expected, and it is only later that further analysis takes place on the breakdown of the figures.

One important factor to examine is the level of exports and imports. An increase in imports that is sustained over a long period is particularly worrying, especially if it is accompanied by a long-term decrease in exports. It is also important to examine the volume figures for both exports and imports. If nothing else this extracts the effects on the balance of payments of relative price changes. For example, if the US dollar falls against the pound sterling, then if the volume of UK exports to the US remains the same, the value of these exports will fall, with a consequent worsening of the trade position, assuming that exporters make changes in their dollar prices.

However, one of the most important things of all is to look at past revisions. Normally, the market only concentrates on the preceding month, but in the past there have often been times when revisions have continued for several years. These tend to have little effect, presumably because they are replacing figures that were in the capital accounts or adjustments, and the market feels they have already been allowed for.

2. Invisible trade

Invisibles are made up of such factors as earnings from banking, insurance and tourism. They also include interest and dividend payments that cross borders, and government transfers. Many of these are impossible to measure, and are very difficult even to estimate. Consequently, revisions tend to take place over a very long period. This also means that figures are usually only produced quarterly, and not on a monthly basis. In the UK, the figure that is used for invisibles when the monthly trade figures are announced is merely a projection based on recent trends. In the case of the USA, the figures are only produced quarterly at some time after the end of the quarter. Consequently, they tend to have a much more muted effect in the USA than in the UK.

3. Current account

This is obviously the balance of visibles and invisibles. For the same reasons as outlined above, it tends to be the most important in the UK. However, this also reflects the fact that on a proportional basis invisibles are much more important to the UK than many other countries, the USA included.

However, theory would suggest that it is the current account figure that is most relevant when assessing the impact of flows on an exchange rate, but because of reporting inaccuracies and delays, the balance of trade figure is a much more usual proxy in the foreign exchange market.

4. Capital account

The capital account covers a wide range of items, some of which are relatively easy to identify, and others which are impossible to measure. In other words the same problems arise as in the measurement of invisibles, except that they are several times worse.

The first major area, and one that is quite easy to estimate is direct investment, both inward and outward. This would cover such things as equity investment, investment in bonds, or investment in new plant. The second area is that of money market investment. This can be picked up to some extent through the monetary statistics for money inward, but it is much more difficult to measure money flows outward. The final area can be the most important at times and yet is well nigh impossible to measure; it is the leads and lags associated with current account flows. This is where a company uses forward cover to hedge an expected import or export. At the time of cover there is a capital flow in one direction which will be matched and replaced by a subsequent flow of goods measured in the current account. There are really no statistics available, and this type of lead and lag is rarely estimated. Consequently, it results in errors and omissions.

5. Errors and omissions

In the UK this is known somewhat confusingly as the balancing item and is the catch-all which ensures that the balance of payments balances in an accounting sense – which it must do as it is a double-entry book-keeping system. Some idea of the accuracy of the remainder of the balance of payments statistics can be judged by the size and volatility of this figure. In recent times it has frequently been very big and very volatile.

6. Overall balance of payments

If we add all the constituent parts together we get the overall balance of payments. If a currency is totally free floating, then these figures will sum to zero. If not, then there will be an official financing figure which will represent the level of intervention.

7. Official financing

If a currency is not floating freely, then there will be an overall surplus or deficit on the balance of payments, and this must be counterbalanced by an opposite item here. Typically, this will be a change in the level of gold and foreign currency reserves, or it may be a borrowing or repayment of borrowing from overseas banks, or from the IMF or other such organisation.

8. Summary

The problem with the latter categories listed above (apart from the trade and current account figure), from the foreign exchange markets' point of view, is that they are both inaccurate and subject to much revision, and that they are very much a lagging indicator because they are released well after the flows that have affected the exchange rate. However, it is worth noting that Germany does release monthly capital account figures slightly after the current account figures. There have been times when the foreign exchange market has sold the Deutschmark on a capital account deficit, even though there has been no official intervention, and the market was already aware that there was a current account surplus; a case of mistaken identity if ever there was one.

9. Changes in official reserves

These really tell you little about the balance of payments – although they are part of it. However, they are anxiously awaited at times of intervention in the foreign exchange markets by central banks, because they give a fairly reliable guide to the level of intervention. In most cases the figures are produced on a monthly basis quite soon after the event.

Money supply statistics and interest rates

In the main body of this book a good deal of stress was placed on the importance of interest rates in determining exchange rates, particularly in the short term. The volatility of interest rates has tended to increase over the last few years, and this has given added impetus to their importance. This volatility is a direct product of the rise of monetarism, or at least an understanding of the importance of restricting monetary growth. Therefore it will come as no surprise that the growth in the monetary aggregates has become an important economic release for the foreign exchange markets. The problem, however, is which aggregate is the correct one to examine, and this is usually seen to be the one that the policy makers are examining. After all, this is the most likely indicator to lead to changes in interest rates.

Each country has its own financial institutional framework and monetary definitions are almost unique. It would thus be an enormous task to describe them all. Emphasis will be on the USA and the UK, and no mention will be made of the others, however important they may have been, or may be in the future. First, however, we consider some aspects of monetary policy that are linked to fiscal policy, and do have some common denominator across national boundaries.

1. Budget deficit or surplus

This can itself be divided into two parts:

(a) the forecast for the year; and
(b) regular fiscal updates on, usually, a monthly basis.

The government deficit is important to monetary growth because, together with bank lending, it is the most important component of broad monetary growth. In addition, the need to finance (or fund) changes in the deficit will have a major importance in determining longer-term interest rates by creating an increased supply of long-term assets.

Generally a reducing budgetary deficit is seen as producing lower interest rates. In the long term this is achieved by reducing the supply and hence driving up the price of government bonds as a relative shortage is created. At the short end of the yield curve, interest rates are likely to come down as inflationary fears recede. Government spending in excess of revenue is often seen as a major source of inflation in these monetarist times. This is of course a simplistic view because it ignores important effects such as liquidity preference and risk, but it is the view that the foreign exchange markets often adopt.

The annual budgetary forecast is particularly eagerly awaited, presumably because markets have an almost touching faith in governments being able to keep to their targets. The monthly figures are also important, but the highly seasonal nature of tax flows and government spending makes them difficult to interpret immediately.

2. Treasury bill and bond auctions

Any budget deficit has to be funded in some way, either by borrowing from overseas or non-banks, or by borrowing from banks (or even the central bank) – the so-called printing of money. However, in recent years it has been felt that it is important to neutralise the monetary effect of any budget deficit as far as possible. This means selling the debt to non-banks or overseas. Different methods are used in different parts of the world to sell government debt. For example, in the UK, gilts are usually sold by tap. This means that the Bank of England offers the gilts at a price that changes only now and again. However, in the USA, the approach is quite different.

The authorities will decide what amounts of what maturities are to be offered at a given time, and these amounts then go to auction, with the highest bidders generally getting the stock. The major auctions take place once a quarter, and because they are quite a discrete feature (unlike the UK approach which is more continuous), they have become important indicators as to the course of longer-term interest rates.

Recently there has been a secondary consideration for the foreign exchange market, which has often assumed primary importance. The large government and trade deficits have had to be funded by overseas capital inflows from the surplus countries, in particular the Japanese. Therefore it has become crucial to the dollar to determine how easily capital inflows can be attracted. A very poor showing by overseas investors in the bill and bond auction will suggest that either a lower dollar or higher interest rates or both are required to attract foreign interest in government securities.

3. Money supply

There are far too many definitions of money supply in the major economies for even a partial analysis to be undertaken here. Furthermore, the definitions are continually changing in importance and new definitions are being introduced. However, a few generalisations can usefully be made.

(a) Narrow money

Narrow money is the definition that claims to represent transaction balances, i.e. money that the holder sees as highly liquid. Thus it will include cash and bank cheque accounts. However, financial innovation means that today many other forms of money can be seen as spendable. For example, the introduction of NOW accounts in the USA, which paid interest on cheque accounts meant that M_1 – the narrow definition – understated monetary growth. In the UK, the growth of building society cheque accounts has had a similar effect.

Attempts have been made to widen the narrow definitions in order to take in these changes, but this is a continuously moving feast. In contrast, some monetarists would argue that real monetary control can only be exercised through control of the monetary base – essentially cash and banks' balances at the central bank. Indeed, in the UK the monetary base M0 is at present the chosen aggregate for control.

(b) Broad money

Broad money includes narrow money, but adds to it those assets which can easily be turned into transaction balances. However, it excludes cash in bank tills and bankers' balances at the central bank. If narrow money poses problems in definition caused by changing financial assets, the problems are several times worse for broad money.

The problems are: what does 'easily' mean? How long a delay is acceptable for money still to be useful as a means of exchange? To what extent should the ability to take credit, for example through credit cards, be included in the definition? Add to these problems the fact that in any economy new methods of attracting funds will always be developing, and one is left with an almost insurmountable problem. Consequently, most economies have a large number of broad definitions which are particularly susceptible to being dropped, or coming back into favour. The cynical would tend to say they come into favour when they tell the story that the authorities wish to portray.

If we take the UK as an example, then M_3 (previously sterling M_3) was for a long time the measure that was targeted and watched. This pretty well covered the deposits of the banking system, as well as cash. However, with the deregulation of the building societies, their assets and liabilities became barely distinguishable from those of the banking system. As a result a new definition, M4, incorporated the deposits of the building societies with those of the banks.

Overall, broad money supply in some shape or form is an important indicator for the market in terms of both the level of credit in an economy, and the likely response of the authorities. It is for this reason that the most important measure is usually the one that the authorities are targeting.

4. Short-term liquidity

Short-term liquidity is, by and large, determined by flows between the government sector (in its widest sense) and the remainder of the economy. Thus if a government spends more than it receives, then there will be a surplus of liquidity; and there will be a shortage of liquidity if the reverse occurs. If these imbalances were not counteracted, then there would be periods when the whole system would be short of liquidity, which inevitably would lead to failures of financial institutions. This is clearly not desirable. Thus in most economies the central bank acts as lender of last resort to the financial system, and will do its best to smooth the effect of any imbalance in the flow of funds, which will have the added benefit of smoothing the level of short-term interest rates, but more importantly through this mechanism it enables the authorities to control the level of short-term rates. This is very important for all markets, not least foreign exchange markets, and it is thus important to understand the institutional framework within which this can take place. Whole books have been written about this. Here we will only look briefly at the USA and the UK, picking out some of the more salient features.

(a) The USA

Here the Federal Reserve (Fed) is the key player, particularly the Federal Open Market Committee (FOMC). This group meets once a month to decide policy, and it may have interim telephone contact if circumstances demand it. The minutes of the meeting are published, but with a time lag. In fact the next meeting has taken place before the previous minutes are revealed. Hence the market, while interested in the minutes, which may give some clues to the tenor of the next meeting, will be particularly anxious to gauge what changes in policy may have occurred, but which it will have to guess at for the time being. This is because the Fed's intentions are not always easy to interpret from the data.

The key rates here are the discount rate, and the Federal funds rate. The former is the rate at which the member banks of the Fed can borrow against the security of government paper. However, this is not changed very often, and these days has more of a psychological than any other kind of value. Most adjustment of liquidity is by way of open-market operations.

If the Fed wishes to add liquidity it will undertake 'repos', the purchase of government securities, with an agreement to sell them back at a fixed date in the future. If it wishes to reduce liquidity it will undertake 'matched sales' – which are the reverse of 'repos'. Repos can be of two types: 'system' when the Fed acts on its own account, and 'customer' when it acts on behalf of, typically, an overseas central bank. The effects are the same, but system repos are seen as a stronger signal by the Fed.

The 'Fed funds rate' is the rate at which the funds required by banks to lodge at the Fed as part of their reserve requirements are traded from one bank to another. The rate will obviously fluctuate throughout the day, as payments are made in and out of the system, but the band is fairly narrow. The skill of the analyst is to quickly pick up when the rate is actually being pushed up by the Fed, and is not just a temporary market aberration.

The Fed produces weekly data on its actions and these are widely analysed in the attempt to read the runes of the FOMC's collective mind.

(b) The UK

The system in the UK is very different in that intervention is generally conducted using open-market operations through the medium of the discount houses – a peculiarly British group of institutions. Instead of relieving liquidity shortages in the banking system directly through the interbank market, for example, the Bank of England will buy eligible commercial bills from the discount houses. An eligible commercial bill is any bill that has been accepted by an eligible bank – there are some 150 of them.

Each morning the Bank of England announces its estimate of any shortage or surplus in the banking system – the estimate is fairly accurate since the Bank is familiar with the flows to and from the public or government sector. If we assume there is a shortage, then discount houses will be invited to offer bills for sale at a price of their choosing. If this rate is acceptable to the authorities, then the transaction will take place. In the vast majority of cases the rate will be the same as that on the day before; this is announced, and no change in the level of short-term interest rates will occur. The rate at which these transactions are done is known as the intervention rate. There are in fact four of them, each relating to a time-band of bills, but the differences between them are quite minor.

A change in rates can occur in one of two ways. Either the discount houses will correctly alter the price at which they offer bills, in which case the Bank will agree to the deal and the intervention rates will change (this frequently happens after prompting or an announcement by the Bank that it intends to change the intervention rates). Alternatively, the Bank may by-pass open-market operations completely, turn down all offers of bills, and lend directly to the discount houses as lender of last resort at a rate of its choosing. If this second mechanism is used the intervention rates will change the following

day. Generally, changes in interest rates are announced between 12 noon and
12.30 p.m., but when a strong signal is intended, the announcement may well
occur at 10.00 a.m. or soon thereafter.

Leading indicators

The idea of a leading indicator is that it predicts how the economy will move
in, say, the next six months. As such it is generally formed by an average (often
weighted) of a number of indicators that have in the past been good predictors
of the economic cycle. An obvious objection to their use is that they are an
extrapolation of the past only, and there is no guarantee that the future will be
the same.

Such series are available in a number of countries, but it is in the USA that
the technique is most developed; and it is only *this* leading indicator, which is a
monthly series, that the market is really interested in. Indeed, it has been quite
a good predictor over long periods, and the objection noted above is somewhat
less valid.

However, other objections do stand up. The series is now based on 11
indicators – for example stock prices, real money supply, the average working
week and building permits. But only nine of these are available at the time of
publication, so the series is often subject to quite large revisions.

There is also a certain amount of folklore attached. For example three
consecutive monthly declines is said to lead always to recession. This despite
the fact that some declines may be very small indeed and may be subject to
upward revision later.

However, although these objectives may be real, there is no doubt that the
foreign exchange market does believe in the efficacy of the US leading
indicator.

INDEX

INDEX